WANTED:

Frank & Jesse James

THE REAL STORY

Dedication

I dedicate this book to D. R. Smith and Ray Puechner.
One gave me a push . . . the other a shove.

MARGARET BALDWIN

To Jackson County, Missouri . . . Its Past and Present

PAT O'BRIEN

There has been some confusion over the years concerning the spelling of the name of Jesse James's stepfather, Dr. Reuben Samuel. The name was actually spelled *Samuel*. According to Milt Perry, curator of the James Farm in Kearney, Missouri, the name was pronounced *Samuels*. Homer Croy, who lived in the neighborhood, began the practice of spelling the name as it was pronounced. More scholarly writers, such as Dr. William Settle, spell the name without the "*s*." Since I wanted to impart the flavor of the times and the surroundings of the James family in my book, I followed the old Missouri tradition of spelling the name with the "*s*." —Margaret Baldwin

WANTED:

Frank & Jesse James

THE REAL STORY

Margaret Baldwin and Pat O'Brien

JULIAN MESSNER
NEW YORK

Published by Julian Messner, a Simon & Schuster
Division of Gulf & Western Corporation,
Simon & Schuster Building,
1230 Avenue of the Americas,
New York, New York 10020.
JULIAN MESSNER and colophon are trademarks of
Simon & Schuster.

Manufactured in the United States of America.
Third printing, 1983
Design by Irving Perkins Associates

Picture Credits: Jackson County Historical Society,
Independence, Missouri

Missouri State Historical Society,
Robert Baldwin

Library of Congress Cataloging in Publication Data
Baldwin, Margaret, 1948-
Wanted, Frank & Jesse James.

Bibliography: p.
Includes index.
Summary: A biography of the notorious outlaw
brothers who fought as Confederate guerillas
during the Civil War and led a gang of bank and
train robbers during the late 1860's and 1870's
    1. James, Jesse,1847–1882—Juvenile literature.
2. James, Frank, 1844–1915—Juvenile literature.
3. Frontier and pioneer life—West (U.S.)—Juvenile
literature. 4. West (U.S.)—History—1860–1880—
Juvenile literature. 5. Outlaws—West (U.S.)—
Biography—Juvenile literature. 6. West (U.S.)—
Biography—Juvenile literature. [1. James,
Jesse, 1847–1882. 2. James, Frank, 1844–1915.
3. Robbers and outlaws. 4. West (U.S.)—Biography.
5. Frontier and pioneer life—West (U.S.)]
I. O'Brien, Pat. II. Title. III. Title: Wanted,
Frank and Jesse James.
F594.J25B34   978'.02'0922 [B] [920]   81–11293
ISBN 0-671-34060-3   AACR2

Acknowledgments

We wish to acknowledge the work of the following two authors whose books present accurate, in-depth studies of the civil war in Missouri and the James brothers: Richard S. Brownlee, *Gray Ghosts of the Confederacy,* Louisiana State University Press, Baton Rouge, Louisiana, 1958; and William A. Settle, Jr., *Jesse James Was His Name,* University of Nebraska Press, Lincoln, Nebraska, 1966 (Bison Book Edition, 1977, published by arrangement with the University of Missouri Press). We wish to also acknowledge the use of *The Trial of Frank James for Murder,* A Jingle Bob Facsimile Edition, with an introduction by James D. Horan, Crown Publishers, New York, 1977, and *Jesse James Was My Neighbor* by Homer Croy, Duell, Sloan and Pearce, New York, 1949.

Local historian Milton Perry of Clay County, Missouri, in charge of the restoration of the James Farm in Kearney, Missouri, provided us with much valuable help, as did Jack Wymore of the Jesse James Bank Museum in Liberty, Missouri. Our thanks to Donald R. Hale and his self-published books titled, *We Rode With Quantrill* and *They Called Him Bloody Bill: The Missouri Badman who Taught Jesse James Outlawry,* 1975, Independence, Missouri.

Special thanks to the Jackson County Historical Society and Nancy Ehrlich for taking time to help us; to Missouri author, Gertrude Bell, for her grandfather's quote on the Civil War in Missouri; to the City of Independence and Herald Publishing House where we are employed; to our families and friends who now know more about Jesse than they ever expected!

Margaret Baldwin
Pat O'Brien

The people they did say,
For many miles away,
The bank was robbed by Frank and Jesse James.

—*The Ballad of Jesse James*

Contents

PROCLAMATION

OF THE

GOVERNOR OF MISSOURI!

REWARDS

FOR THE ARREST OF

Express and Train Robbers.

STATE OF MISSOURI,
EXECUTIVE DEPARTMENT.

WHEREAS, It has been made known to me, as the Governor of the State of Missouri, that certain parties, whose names are to me unknown, have confederated and banded themselves together for the purpose of committing robberies and other depredations within this State; and

WHEREAS, Said parties did, on or about the Eighth day of October, 1879, stop a train near Glendale, in the county of Jackson, in said State, and, with force and violence, take, steal and carry away the money and other express matter being carried thereon; and

WHEREAS, On the fifteenth day of July, 1881, said parties and their confederates did stop a train upon the line of the Chicago, Rock Island and Pacific Railroad, near Winston, in the County of Daviess, in said State, and, with force and violence, take, steal, and carry away the money and other express matter being carried thereon; and, in perpetration of the robbery last aforesaid, the parties engaged therein did kill and murder one WILLIAM WESTFALL, the conductor of the train, together with one JOHN McCULLOCH, who was at the time in the employ of said company, then on said train; and

WHEREAS, FRANK JAMES and JESSE W. JAMES stand indicted in the Circuit Court of said Daviess County, for the murder of JOHN W. SHEETS, and the parties engaged in the robberies and murders aforesaid have fled from justice and have absconded and secreted themselves:

NOW, THEREFORE, in consideration of the premises, and in lieu of all other rewards heretofore offered for the arrest or conviction of the parties aforesaid, or either of them, by any person or corporation, I, THOMAS T. CRITTENDEN, Governor of the State of Missouri, do hereby offer a reward of five thousand dollars ($5,000.00) for the arrest and conviction of each person participating in either of the robberies or murders aforesaid, excepting the said FRANK JAMES and JESSE W. JAMES; and, for the arrest and delivery of said

FRANK JAMES and JESSE W. JAMES,

and each or either of them, to the sheriff of said Daviess County, I hereby offer a reward of five thousand dollars, ($5,000.00,) and for the conviction of either of the parties last aforesaid of participation in either of the murders or robberies above mentioned, I hereby offer a further reward of five thousand dollars, ($5,000.00,)

IN TESTIMONY WHEREOF, I have hereunto set my hand and caused to be affixed the Great Seal of the State of Missouri. Done

[SEAL.]   at the City of Jefferson on this 28th day of July, A. D. 1881.

THOS. T. CRITTENDEN.

By the Governor:

MICH'L K. McGRATH, Sec'y of State.

State Hist. Soc. of Mo.

Introduction

by Margaret Baldwin

Frank and Jesse James were gun-slinging, murdering robbers. They were born in Missouri, when it was the edge of civilization in America. They were guerrillas in the Civil War, one of the most violent conflicts ever fought, and they participated in the most vicious part of that war—the battle on the Missouri and Kansas border. Their contemporaries were Wild Bill Hickok, Billy the Kid, Wyatt Earp, Doc Holliday, the Dalton brothers, and John Wesley Hardin. Yet none of these men attained the worldwide legendary status of the James brothers. These two outlaws became symbols of the fight against oppression and injustice to hundreds of people and as such they are romanticized in story and song.

The real lives of the brothers have been distorted. Dime novels of the times related hundreds of wild tales about them. Jesse has died at the hands of Bob Ford countless times on the stage and screen. Unfortunately, most of what has been portrayed about "the boys" is the product of active imaginations. Thus the true story of the violent era they rode out of that turned them into heroes, and the legacy of hatred and bitterness it left behind, has been forgotten. Besides, as Sherlock Holmes said, "for strange effects and extraordinary combinations we must go to life itself, which is always far more daring than any effort of the imagination." The real lives of the brothers are far more fascinating than any dime novel!

Why do such men deserve biographies?

Because they did become symbols to people whose homes

had been torn apart by the war, people who were trying to survive in a wrecked economy and who felt that they had lost control of their lives to a nameless system. Frank and Jesse, by robbing banks and holding up trains, were striking back at that system. They became symbols to their people in the same way Robin Hood was in a period of injustice and turmoil in Great Britain.

To understand the James brothers and what they represented to people, it is necessary to understand the terrible border wars—the inglorious part of the Civil War that is often forgotten. "Those who do not study history are doomed to repeat it." Frank and Jesse James lived through a tragic time in our nation's history, a time of violence that continued to spawn violence in a chaotic society long after the Stars and Bars were lowered in defeat. This period needs to be remembered time and again.

Our hope is that we are not doomed to repeat it.

PART I

The Border Wars

... the law spoke too softly to be heard in such a noise of war.
—PLUTARCH

In this war, both sides lost.
—OLD MISSOURIAN

A column of Union cavalry trots along a dusty path past a green and leafy forest, the brush, one summer's day in Missouri. Birds sing and whistle, chatter and caw. The nervous scouts constantly peer into the wilderness, but see nothing except the dark, moving shadows of the trees. A breeze lifts the branches, cools the riders, and blows little swirls of dust down the path.

Suddenly the cavalry is horrified to hear a most inhuman sound coming from human throats—the rebel yell. Men on horseback dash out of the brush, shooting with deadly accuracy at the orderly column of uniformed soldiers. Within moments, they are gone, leaving behind Union dead and wounded. Most never got to fire a shot. The dazed and furious soldiers plunge into the brush, only to find that the brush protects her own. Weeds four feet high grow so thickly a horse can only break its way through with strenuous, wearing effort. Scrub trees, pine and walnut, stick up sharply out of the weeds, tearing flesh and clothing. Vicious vines twine around the undergrowth and unwary horses' hooves. Gullies open up, wide chasms of dying vegetation and fallen logs. The soldiers turn their horses this way and that, but they have been defeated by the brush and by an enemy that has galloped off in fifty different directions. The guerrillas know the paths.

They know the brush.

Chapter One

The Reverend Mr. James

In 1841 a quiet, dark-haired young college student married a tall, strong-willed young woman from a Catholic seminary in Lexington, Kentucky. The groom, Robert Sallee James, was preparing himself for the ministry. He was twenty-three years old. The bride, Zerelda Cole, was only sixteen. Robert met her while attending Georgetown College. She was living in a Catholic seminary, where she had been placed by a guardian uncle following her father's death and her mother's remarriage.

Robert James' grandparents had arrived in America from England and were married in 1774. By 1805 they were living in

Jesse Woodson James, age 16.

Goochland County, Virginia, where William James was a prosperous landowner. When he died in that year, he left his widow and her sons with land holdings in three counties. Their personal property also included slaves.

The oldest boy, John, born in 1775, married Mary Poor in 1807 in Goochland County. They moved to Logan County, Kentucky, in 1811 with other members of the family. The family prospered until John and Mary died suddenly, within a few months of each other, in 1827, leaving seven minor children in the care of the oldest girl, Mary, who was just eighteen herself. Robert James was only nine years old when his parents died. He was raised by his sister, who married John Mimms in 1828. In addition to raising Mary's brothers and sisters, the Mimms had five children of their own. One of these children, Zee Mimms, would later become the wife of her own first cousin, Jesse James, son of Robert and Zerelda.

Relatives may have tried to persuade the young couple to wait awhile before they married, because Zerelda was so young. But she was a determined young woman with a fiery temper. It was not pleasant to cross her, and the marriage proceeded. The newlyweds were not troubled by financial worries. The groom put up a bond of fifty pounds of tobacco to seal his marriage commitment and Zerelda told in later years that she

Zerelda Cole (James) Samuels, mother of the James brothers.

was given "two slaves and six thousand dollars" for a wedding present. (She may have meant "two slaves worth six thousand dollars." This would seem more likely.)

Following Robert's graduation and ordination to the ministry, the young couple decided to travel to Clay County, Missouri, where Zerelda's mother was living. They were embarking upon a real adventure, because Missouri was considered the last outpost of civilization. Beyond was the forbidding prairie and Indian territory. The land was young and wild, having been settled in the 1830s. Independence, Missouri, Jackson County, across the Missouri river, was the outfitting center for wagon trains heading west to Sante Fe, California and Oregon. River trade caused other towns to spring up like mushrooms along the banks of the Missouri. One town came close to calling itself Possum Trot, but eventually decided upon the more respectable Kansas City.

The Baptist church was just gaining a foothold in the formerly wild frontier towns that were now filling with families fleeing the overpopulated industrialized cities. The church welcomed the young minister James and his new bride.

Old-timers remembered the Reverend Mr. James as a powerful speaker and dedicated worker. He was a sincerely good man who was well-liked by his neighbors. "Robert James was the best man I ever knew," one recalled. A portrait of the minister, hanging in the James home in Kearney, Missouri, shows a thin, handsome man with dark hair, a pale, narrow face, and dark eyes that must have burned with religious zeal when he preached. He was quiet and studious. This was in sharp contrast to his high-spirited wife who was already getting a reputation as a sharp-tongued woman with a hair-trigger temper. The two apparently complemented each other, however, for they were a devoted couple. Robert was popular with the people in the area. He took over the New Hope Baptist Church, reorganized it, and increased the membership. He also is credited with starting two other congregations.

Life was bright and full of promise for the young couple, and their happiness increased with the birth of a son on January 10, 1843. He was christened Alexander Franklin James. Another child, Robert, was born in 1845, but he died in infancy. Little Frank was four years old when another boy, named Jesse Woodson James, was born on September 5, 1847. A girl, Susan Levenia, was born in 1849.

Robert started his children's education at an early age, an unusual thing for most frontier parents, but Robert James was a strong believer in education. Most settlers believed that children should be taught to read the Bible, write their names, and learn to shoot and plow straight. Girls were taught to cook, keep house, sew, and raise children. But already, more advanced members of the frontier communities knew that the day would come when some of the young people would demand the benefits of higher education and leave home to find it unless colleges were provided.

Robert James joined with General Alexander Doniphan, a hero in the Mexican wars and a highly respected man in the community, in a drive to obtain a Baptist college for Liberty, Missouri, in Clay County. The college was originally planned for a town nearer the center of the state, but Doniphan marshaled his religious forces with the same skill he handled his military ones, and Liberty was chosen for the site of what would become William Jewell College. The Reverend Robert James is recorded as one of its first trustees. No doubt he dreamed of one day seeing his own sons graduate from the young college.

Robert James' life was progressing well. Already he was becoming a high-ranking member of his community. His future success appeared to be unlimited. But an obsession was sweeping the land, and it caught the frontier preacher in its deathly grip.

Chapter Two

Gold Fever

Robert James was a prosperous man by 1850. He held unencumbered title to 275 acres of land that he farmed with the help of seven slaves. He built a house with slave quarters and a barn. He owned sheep, cattle, three horses, and a yoke of oxen. His estate also included more than fifty books on subjects of such wide variety as chemistry, theology, Shakespeare, literature, and public speaking. He was respected and well-liked in the community and the future for the young minister looked bright.

But then gold fever swept the country. It struck full force in 1848 and 1849, when word of the Sutter's Mill strike leaked out. Incredible accounts of untold fortunes made in days, sometimes even hours, came filtering through from the west coast. The men of the Missouri frontier towns were particularly affected by the news. Most were adventurers who had traveled to Missouri seeking their fortunes. They had no deep and lasting roots in the state and were therefore eager to gamble for higher stakes by making another overland journey. They had direct access to all the necessities for their travels, since Independence in nearby Jackson County had been outfitting people for overland crossings since 1830. A group of Clay County men left almost immediately in 1849, and an even larger number of gold-seekers left in 1850, despite stories of a serious outbreak of cholera in the mining camps. The Reverend Robert James was among this last group.

James brothers and comrade during Civil War. Frank is seated. Jesse is standing to Frank's left. Fletcher Taylor is on the right.

Dime-novels portrayed the preacher's departure as that of a wealth-hungry man abandoning his wife and children. Robert James' greedy nature was born again in his sons and led them to a life of crime. Others related dark rumors that the minister was driven from his home by his evil wife, who broke his heart by running around with wild men. Some said her violent temper made James' life unbearable. But evidence found by modern scholars indicates that Robert's leaving for the gold fields was neither sinister nor romantic.

The young minister's letters home during his absence, reveal a deep love and longing for his family. In one letter he sends his regards to his friends and concludes with "kiss little Jesse for me and bid Franklin be a good boy and learn fast." He wrote of his efforts to find Clay County men who had left earlier, to give them messages from their families. He apparently did not go seeking gold, since he tried panning only once during the entire time he was there. He may have gone to California simply to shepherd his flock. He may also have gone to visit a brother, Drury James, living in California. He wrote to his family of returning in about a year.

But the man of God soon realized that he would never see his family again. Perhaps he had a premonition of approaching death, or perhaps he was already in the grips of the disease that killed him, for one letter to his wife reads, "pray for me that if no more (we) meet in this world we can meet in Glory." Within a few weeks of his arrival in California, the frontier preacher, Robert James, died and was buried in an unmarked grave. He was only thirty-two years old. He left behind a twenty-five-year-old widow and three small children.

In later years, the old-timers often said that life for the James boys would have been different if their father had lived. But it was the Civil War that influenced the James boys, as it destroyed or changed many lives then. Robert James, quiet, God-fearing man though he was, could not have escaped its terror. There is no doubt, either, about which side the preacher would have supported. He was a Kentuckian and a slave-owner. He most certainly would have urged his sons to fight for the Confederacy, as they eventually did.

Robert James left his family and died far from home. It is told that when the young minister stepped out of his door, little Jesse clung to his knees and begged his father not to go. Robert looked down at the three-year-old child and very nearly changed his mind. But he said to his wife that he had given "his word he would go, and a man could never go back on his word." He walked away, leaving Jesse crying in his mother's arms.

William Clarke Quantrill

Chapter Three

Frank Joins Quantrill

Zerelda remarried following her husband's death. The young widow needed help running the farm and providing for her three children. Her second husband's name was Benjamin Simms. He was considerably older than Zerelda and they were together only a few months before he packed up and moved out. He died shortly after. Family tradition maintains that Simms was cruel to Zerelda's boys, but a few of the old-timers whisper that the boys tormented the man until they drove him away. No one knows the truth, but Frank and Jesse did get along well with their mother's third husband.

In 1855 Zerelda married Dr. Reuben Samuels. She was thirty and he was twenty-six. Frank was twelve and Jesse eight when their new stepfather moved in. Samuels was a physician, but he apparently enjoyed farming more than "doctoring," since he spent most of his time working the land. It was another marriage of opposites. Dr. Samuels was remembered as quiet and gentle. One reason he got along well with Zerelda's boys, rumor says, was because he didn't try to discipline them. Zerelda herself was well known throughout the community for her violent temper and outspoken pro-Southern opinions. Neighbors described them as a devoted couple, however, and Frank and Jesse soon had four half-brothers and sisters to play with, along with their own sister, Susie.

The boys attended the Prairie Grove school during the winter, helping with farm chores in their spare time. In the sum-

26

Frank James,
age 23.

mers they plowed and tended crops, fished and hunted. Most boys of the time were proficient with guns, and if the family could afford one, that meant free meat on the table. The entire family attended the Baptist church in Kearney every Sunday. Jesse, especially, enjoyed church services. He was devoutly religious as a young boy. One story the old-timers tell is about the Sunday young Jesse stood up and prayed for the soul of his older brother, Frank, who wasn't much of a church-goer. Jesse was fun-loving and sociable. He enjoyed being with people and made friends easily. He had one serious fault, however. He had inherited his mother's violent temper. Jesse also hadn't much use for "book-learnin'."

Frank took after his late father. He even resembled him physically. He remembered his father's early educational training and loved to read the books left in Robert James' library, especially Shakespeare. The boy was quiet and kept to himself more than Jesse. He was a "doubter," people said, when it came to his father's religion and remained one all his life. Both boys were hard-workers, and not known as troublemakers. Times were hard and getting worse for the border towns where they lived.

Years before the Civil War officially began with the firing on Fort Sumter, border warfare had broken out on the Kansas-Missouri border. Missourians, most of whom had ties with the South, had always expected Kansas to enter the Union as a slave state. Northern abolitionists poured men and money into Kansas to swing the vote to a free state. This infuriated the Missourians and, consequently, each side sent armed raiding parties to the other side to "explain" their political views. This was still frontier territory. Men were accustomed to settling questions at gunpoint and politics was no exception.

Frank and Jesse were raised in an atmosphere of turmoil and hatred. Neighbor argued with neighbor, husband with wife, brother with brother. Although Southern in background, most Missourians were opposed to secession; Missouri was the only state in the Union the moderate Douglas carried. But her governor was Southern and wanted Missouri to be another Confederate star. The state was ripped apart. The area Frank and Jesse lived in was, for the most part, pro-Southern, although Kansas City was a Union town. The fiery Zerelda was violently pro-Southern. When General Sterling Price of the Confederate army came to Clay County on a recruiting drive after war had been declared, eighteen-year-old Frank James was one of the first to join. Thirteen-year-old Jesse watched enviously as his brother marched off to war.

Frank fought in the Battle of Wilson's Creek, one of the first major Midwestern battles, in the summer of 1861. The rebels won that battle and marched north to fight at Lexington. The

Union army forced them south again and eventually Price's army ended up in Arkansas. Frank was not with them. He caught the measles and was left behind in a hospital in Springfield, Missouri. When Union troops overran the hospital, Frank was paroled and allowed to return home. Like so many other young men his age, he was a soldier without an army.

The border warfare escalated once the national battle lines had been drawn. Union troops from Kansas had official authority to raid Missouri. One of the worst offenders was "Doc" Jennison, who joined the Union army and was appointed to a command position. One of Jennison's raids had far-reaching effects on the future lives of the James'. Jennison and his men rode into Harrisonville, Missouri, and robbed and looted the town. One wealthy Jackson County stock raiser and farmer had over four thousand dollars in carriages, wagons, and harness stolen, as well as forty horses from his livery stable. The man was Colonel Henry Younger, a man who had, ironically, spoken out bitterly against the division of the Union. Only a few months later, Union soldiers would murder Colonel Younger as he traveled in his carriage from an auction, stealing the money he carried. This tragic event changed forever the lives of Henry Younger's sons, Cole, Bob, and Jim.

Because of raids like Jennison's and the fact that young men like Frank James, who supported the Southern cause, had no army to fight with since Price had been forced south, it was natural for guerrilla resistance bands to develop. All that the men required was a leader, and they soon had one. His name was William Quantrill, one of the strangest figures ever to come out of the war, a man who never rose above the rank of colonel (some say he never achieved that officially) but who is as well known as many generals.

A former schoolteacher from Kansas, Quantrill's past life is shrouded in mystery and shadow. He lived for a time with the Indians, where he may have learned the rudiments of guerrilla

William Quantrill in Confederate uniform, around 1862.

warfare. He arrived in Western Missouri early in the 1860s, fought at Lexington with Price, and in the winter of 1861 organized a small band of young men to counter Kansas raids. One of the first to join was the embittered Cole Younger who, one of the old-timers remembers, could not even shoot a pistol and spent every spare minute practicing. The guerrillas burned bridges, attacked small Union patrols, tore up miles of telegraph wire, raided towns along the Kansas border, and made life miserable for the Union command. It is believed that, at one time, over 80,000 Union soldiers were tied up in northwestern Missouri by Quantrill, whose strength averaged between 50 and 250 men.

The date Frank James "took to the brush" to ride with Quantrill is unknown. He was home in May. His name appears on a list of Clay County men who posted a $1,000 bond and took the loyalty oath that month. It is likely Frank joined in the summer of 1862. He was arrested for parole violation at least once and maybe twice. One story says Frank escaped from prison and crossed the river into Jackson County, Quantrill's headquarters, that summer.

"Frank James was the quietest man I ever knew," an old guerrilla fighter recalled. The nineteen-year-old man, always

William Quantrill

less sociable than his brother Jesse, often went for days without saying a word. He enjoyed the men's company and sat listening to the yarns and tall tales, but never contributed much himself.

"When I joined Quantrill's men," Frank recalled, "I was surprised to see them shoot a volley and then turn quickly about on their horses and run the other way into the brush. . . . I was a reckless daredevil like the rest of them, but I must have had my head swelled just a little when I joined Quantrill. I soon had the conceit taken out of me though. One day we were skirmishing with some Federals and I got excited and waved my hat in the air, yelling 'Come on, you Yankee sons of guns.' Just then, an old-time bushwhacker said to me, 'Never mind that sonny. They're coming fast enough. You don't have to hurry them. . . .' "

The average age of the bushwhackers was between seventeen and twenty. Most were too young to grow beards, so they wore their hair in long, flowing curls to their shoulders after the fashion of the plainsmen. Their uniform consisted of a "guerrilla shirt," an open-front, homespun shirt that had four large pockets for carrying ammunition and the cylinders of the Colt.44s, their standard weapon. These shirts were colorfully

31

Captain "Bloody Bill"
Anderson

embroidered by wives, sisters, and mothers. Later, "Bloody
Bill" Anderson's men started adding human scalps to theirs. A
wide-brimmed, slouch hat, worn pinned up on one side, gave
the men a rakish appearance. Each man carried a Sharps rifle
or a shotgun on his saddle and numerous Colt revolvers. Bill
Anderson rode with eight Colts stuck in his belt and at least
four more in his saddlebags. Frank James only carried two. He
was a tall, slender boy and said too many guns weighed him
down.

One of the guerrilla fighters recalled Frank James' experience following a fight at a farm near Pleasant Hill, Missouri.
The guerrillas held out against a Union patrol until they were
outnumbered badly by Yankee reinforcements. Quantrill's
usual command at this point was "take to the brush and every
man for himself." When the order came to disperse, Frank
couldn't reach his horse and had to run off without one. He ran
until he came to a vacant barnyard. There stood an old white
mare in a pen with some mules. The mare was ancient, but

Frank was exhausted and anything with four legs looked good. He hopped on her back and started off into the darkness. Then the moon rose. The white mare showed up against the black brush with astonishing brilliance. Frank imagined hundreds of Yankees staring at him on his moonlit mount, and he was just about to abandon his horse when he heard hoofbeats galloping after him. Try as he might, he couldn't convince the old horse to make a fast getaway. The youngster knew his end was near and was just about to dismount and die fighting when he was surrounded by all the mules from the barnyard who had decided to accompany their friend on her travels! Frank soon found himself a better horse.

Chapter Four

Frank James to the Rescue!

Frank stayed with Quantrill, following him into Arkansas during the winter of 1862–63. While in Arkansas, Quantrill and his men joined up with the regular Confederate army under the command of General Tom Hindman. The guerrillas had attained quite a reputation in Missouri for fighting hard and recklessly. They fought under the "black flag," which meant that they took no prisoners. Hindman admired the guerrillas and welcomed them to his forces, which were, for the most part, poorly equipped and half-starved. He assigned the guerrillas to the dashing Jo Shelby, an inspired choice. Shelby was thirty-two and had already made a name for himself as a daring cavalry officer. He suited the guerrilla's style and they all came to admire him.

Shelby would play an important role in the lives of Frank and Jesse James, all because of an incident that occurred in Arkansas that winter during the Battle of Prairie Grove.

Shelby's Iron Brigade, along with the guerrillas, attacked a company of sleeping Missouri cavalry at sunrise on December 7, 1862. The cold soldiers woke to the sound of gunfire and the rebel yell and fled to the rear without firing a shot. Here a major stopped them and angrily ordered them to take a stand. He withdrew his men into a wheat field to await Shelby.

Jo Shelby led the charge, then fell back among the main body of his men urging them on. But he urged them a little too energetically. Glancing around, he suddenly realized that he was alone on the field of battle with only his staff officers near him. His men and the guerrillas had all galloped off in pursuit of the retreating bluecoats. The Union major marched into view, leading a regiment of cavalry. It was six to one hundred.

"You are surrounded and overpowered, sir," shouted the major. "Surrender or I fire."

As Shelby paused, considering whether he should die fighting or in a Yankee prison, he looked up to see Quantrill's guerrillas dashing behind Hubbard's regiment. One of the men riding wildly in front of the desperate-looking group was Frank James. Shelby never forgot that moment.

The guerrillas returned to Missouri in the spring of 1863. It

Jesse W. James at 17. Note the guerrilla shirt. Photo was taken at the time James was riding with the notorious guerrilla leader, Bill Anderson.

would be the most terrible summer in Missouri-Kansas history, culminating in the infamous raid on Lawrence, Kansas.

The guerrillas kept the border in flames that summer. At one point, the newspapers reported Kansas City was completely cut off from the rest of the state by the guerrilla bands. The Union command grew desperate to get rid of Quantrill and his men. They began arresting the female relatives of the known guerrillas, throwing them in prisons until every prison for miles around was filled with old mothers, little sisters, girl-friends, and wives. (Frank's mother spent time in prison as did his little sister, Susie.) This ended in tragedy. A building housing some of the women in Kansas City collapsed under suspicious circumstances, killing several young girls and critically injuring others. One of those killed was Bill Anderson's sister. It is said he stood over her grave and vowed that every Yankee he met would die. From that day, Bloody Bill became little more than a raving maniac.

Rumors spread that all guerrillas and their families would be forced to leave the area; their homes and property confiscated. As one of the men said solemnly, "We could stand no more." They decided to raid Lawrence, Kansas, long known to be a stronghold for Northern guerrillas, such as "Doc" Jennison and the "Grim Chieftan," Jim Lane. Under Quantrill's command, over 400 guerrillas galloped into the sleeping town on August 23, 1863. Quantrill's final order was "Death to every man. Kill every man big enough to carry a gun. But no man is to harm a woman or young child on the pain of death."

Frank James was in the deadly band. So was Cole Younger. Jesse James was not, according to Frank. The guerrillas carried lists of names of known Union men. They went to those houses first and dragged the men out and shot them. Then they began wholesale raiding and looting. They broke into bars, got roaring drunk, and terrorized the townspeople. They set fire to homes and filled wagons with loot to take back to Missouri. Too late, Quantrill realized his men were out of his control. At

9:00 A.M. he received word from his scouts that Union troops were on the way. He had been prepared to fight his way back to Missouri, but he had not counted on the alarming fact that most of his men were now staggering and reeling in the streets. By the sheer force of his own will, this captain, only in his twenties himself, managed to get his men together and started out of town. They left behind one hundred and fifty men and boys dead, one hundred and eighty-five buildings in flames— but not one woman or young child had been molested or injured. Bloody Bill Anderson claimed to have shot eighteen men personally. Frank James and Cole Younger each admitted to shooting several. Only one guerrilla died in Lawrence— a man who was so drunk he mistakenly rode back into town after the others left. It is said an angry mob tore his body apart and left him in the streets, unburied.

The guerrillas escaped back to Missouri, but it was a running fight. Quantrill eventually ordered that the next man who broke ranks would be shot. Once there, they dispersed into the friendly shadows of the brush. But their terrible act of violence would rock the nation and bring about even more death and destruction on the border as the Union retaliated with the infamous Order Number Eleven that ordered all Southern sympathizers to leave Missouri and left three entire counties burned to a no-man's land.

Chapter Five

Jesse Rides with Bloody Bill

The James family lived in Clay County and were not affected by Order Number Eleven. But an incident occurred, probably around this time, that was to burn itself into Jesse's mind and eventually drive him into the brush to join his brother.

Both Zerelda and Jesse had long been suspected by the Union authorities of aiding the guerrillas and acting as messengers and spies. Frank James was also a well-known member of Quantrill's band. One day Union troops rode into the yard of the Samuels' farm. Jesse was plowing the fields, but Dr. Samuels, Zerelda, and the younger children were working in the house. The soldiers shouted for Dr. Samuels to come out into the yard. When he did, they began questioning him about Frank's whereabouts, wanting to know where Quantrill was camped. Dr. Samuels told them he didn't know. The soldiers threatened and abused him, but he still refused to tell. Finally the Union men threw a rope over the limb of a tree, made a noose, and grabbed Dr. Samuels. They dragged him to the foot of the tree, put the noose over his head, then slowly hoisted him off the ground until he was hanging by the neck. Zerelda ran at the soldiers like a wildcat, beating on them and begging them to spare her husband. They knocked her down, although she was expecting another child at the time. When Dr. Samuels lost consciousness, the soldiers lowered him to the ground and revived him. Then they asked him again where they could find Frank. Once again he refused to answer, so they put the noose over his head and strung him back up. They repeated this torture four times, the last time they left him hanging and rode out to the fields after Jesse. Zerelda cut her husband down. He was still alive but in pitiful condition. Dr. Samuels carried the scars of the rope burns to the day of his death.

The soldiers found Jesse in the fields. When he refused to answer their questions, they chased him up and down the plowed furrows, slashing at him with their riding whips. When they let him go, he took refuge in his home until his wounds healed, then he left to follow his brother into the brush.

There is no known date for Jesse's entry into the guerrilla ranks. Family legend says he was sixteen years old and Jesse turned sixteen on September 5, 1863.

It is often said that Jesse James rode with Quantrill. This is not precisely true. Jesse joined Quantrill's captain, Bloody Bill Anderson, and rode with him, although Frank continued under Quantrill's command. A violent dispute arose between the two guerrilla leaders, which ended in the bands splitting up and finally Quantrill left altogether, going into seclusion with several friends. In the end, Frank rode under the command of George Todd and Jesse stayed with Bloody Bill.

Jesse's nickname among the guerrillas was Dingus, and there are various versions of how he came by the unusual name. The best relates that, about a week after he'd joined Anderson, the boy was cleaning his revolver when it accidently discharged, shooting off the tip of his middle finger on his left hand. The young boy, who loved singing in the choir and never missed church, stared down at his bleeding hand and yelped, "That's the dod-dingus pistol I ever saw." The old veterans, who would have turned the air blue with profanity, laughed until they rolled on the ground. Years later, Jesse would be identified by that missing tip of his middle finger.

Bloody Bill admired the young boy under his command. He

said of Jesse, "To have no beard, he is the keenest fighter among us." Jesse was thin, like Frank, but lacked his height. His hair was sandy colored and his eyes a striking color of blue. Those who saw him always remembered his eyes. (This may have been because he suffered from a disease then called granulated eyelids, which resulted in an almost constant, rapid blinking. This must have been unnerving for anyone facing him.) His hands have been described as very delicate and sensitive. His face was smooth, his skin so fair Anderson occasionally had him dress as a girl to trap Union soldiers into ambushes.

Jesse fought with Bloody Bill in Missouri in 1864, when the end of the war was nearing and the rebels were getting desperate. He learned to rob banks under Bill's command; the rebels robbed Union banks several times. They once robbed a train as well. Jesse was involved in the Centralia Massacre, where unarmed Union soldiers were lined up on a platform and shot down in cold blood by Bloody Bill and his terrible confederate, Little Archie Clements. Little Archie, it is told, began the practice of scalping his dead, leaving gruesome notes on their bodies. He was also a particular friend of Jesse's.

Jesse was shot in the lungs in August 1864, and was not expected to live. But he was able to rejoin his command in September. At the age of seventeen, Jesse shot and killed a Union major. But the rebels were losing. Price tried to take Missouri, but was defeated soundly and finally at the Battle of Westport, in October 1864. The guerrilla ranks were broken and scattered. Bloody Bill Anderson rode to his death in manical style. His black curls flying, his pistols blazing, he charged a Union squad of 150 men alone, after his men had been shot up in an ambush. The wild, ghostlike Anderson, who had become a legend of terror along the border, died of two bullets in the back of his head, having broken through the line before the Yankees could kill him. Young Jesse watched and remembered the man responsible for Bill's death, Major Samuel Cox. Jesse vowed he would kill Cox if they ever met again, a vow that would later have a major impact on his life.

After Bill's death, Jesse traveled into Texas and spent the winter of 1864 there, although his exact whereabouts were unknown.

Frank James followed Quantrill into Kentucky, where the guerrillas apparently hoped to surrender with regular Confederate forces and escape execution. They skirmished and fought with Northern guerrillas and, occasionally, Yankee troops, although they were disguised in blue uniforms.

Here Quantrill met his death at the hands of a man named Edwin Terrill. The boys were hiding in a barn when they were surprised by Terrill's men. Quantrill's horse bolted at the sound of the gunfire and ran away, leaving his master stranded in the barnyard. Two of the guerrillas came back for their leader, but before Quantrill could reach them safely, he was shot. One bullet hit him in the spine, paralyzing him. He fell into the dust. The two men who returned were killed. Legend says Quantrill raised himself up on one arm and kept firing at the Yankees pursuing his men. He shot and killed several horses at a great distance, causing Union soldiers to compliment him on his accuracy. He surrendered and was carried into a farmhouse.

That night, Frank James and the other men returned under the cover of darkness and tried to persuade their commander to come back with them, but Quantrill refused. He knew he would only slow them down. He told them to surrender where and when they could and made Frank James their lieutenant. He shook each man's hand and told them farewell. William Quantrill died on June 6, 1865. He was twenty-seven years old—the last of the Missouri guerrilla leaders who had served the Confederacy better than it realized.

The war was over. Their leaders were dead. The Confederacy was shattered. But was the war over for Frank and Jesse?

PART II

Frank and Jesse

Jesse stole from the rich—because the poor didn't have any money!

> Jesse raked in the di'mon rings,
> The big gold watches an' the yuther things;
> Jesse divvied 'em then an' thar
> With a cryin' child had lost her mar.
> *Jesse James* by WILLIAM ROSE BENET

Chapter Six

Surrender!

Following Quantrill's death, Frank and the boys made their way to Samuel's Depot, Kentucky, and surrendered to the authorities on July 26, 1865. The man who accepted their surrender, Captain Mead, was described as "a true soldier and a brave man." Mead allowed the former guerrillas to keep their horses and their sidearms until they received official word from the commanding general of the district that the surrender had been accepted.

Jesse spent the winter of 1864–65 somewhere in Texas with George Shepherd, Little Archie Clements, Jim Anderson (Bloody Bill's brother), and Dave Poole. It must have been remote for none of the boys got word that the South was collapsing. When spring returned to the brush in 1865, the boys rode back into Missouri, intent upon picking up the fighting where they had left off.

Border residents were understandably upset over the guerrillas' return. The war had ended for them with Price's defeat at Westport. No one was certain what to do with the guerrillas. Should they be hunted down or allowed to come in and surrender? When word of Lee's surrender to Grant at Appomattox reached Missouri, most of the boys were ready to throw down their weapons and give up the fight if they could be assured of a peaceful life. The military authorities finally promised they would not take action against them, but would not prevent civil authorities from prosecuting. This was good enough for the guerrillas.

One of the first guerrillas in contact with the military was Dave Poole, and he began to make arrangements to bring his men in. A few still held out; among these were Jesse James and Little Archie. But the two agreed to act as bodyguards on the ride into Lexington where the surrender terms were going to be discussed. Jesse rode at the head of the ragged group, carrying a white flag. He and Little Archie waited until the final arrangements were concluded, then they bid their old comrades farewell and turned to ride away. Suddenly the Union army opened fire. Jesse dropped his white flag and turned to fight. He might have realized then that for a few men on both sides, the war would never end.

But the fight did not last long. Jesse, eighteen years old, was shot once again in the right lung, near the scars where he'd been hit the previous August. He slipped off his horse. The horse was shot and fell dead on top of him. The soldiers closed in. Jesse pulled himself out from under the animal and ran for the brush, the soldiers in pursuit. He fired at them, slowing them a little, then continued running. He was bleeding heavily and was forced to stop once and pull off his boots, which had filled with blood. Barely able to lift his revolver, Jesse fired one final shot at the soldiers, then dropped the gun and staggered on. The soldiers abandoned the chase, probably figuring the boy was too far gone to matter. Jesse dragged himself to a creek bed where he collapsed.

He lay there undiscovered all that night, using the creek water to cool his fever. He was in terrible pain from the chest wound. Late the next day, he realized he might never be found and began crawling to a field he could see in the distance. A farmer discovered the boy and took him to a safe refuge where word went out to Little Archie that his friend was in need of help.

Jesse was near death for days, but the grinning Little Archie proved an able medic and the boy continued to live. Word came that the rest of the old guerrilla band had agreed to surrender terms. They all took the loyalty oath with the exception of two men—Little Archie Clements, who stated that he would rather die than ever surrender, and Jesse James.

In later years, the newspapers would print that Jesse, too, had vowed to die rather than give up. But, according to Jesse's family, the boy was too badly injured to ride in with the others and take the oath. Major Rodgers, in command at Lexington, reportedly understood that Jesse had surrendered. Major Rodgers said later that he believed Jesse was dying anyway and would soon be surrendering to a higher authority than his. He stated that he could not bring himself to force the suffering young man to take the loyalty oath.

Rodgers apparently took such pity on the dying boy that he even paid for his transportation to Nebraska where the Samuels were now living. Legend says the family had been driven from Clay County when the fiery-tempered Zerelda was caught trying to choke a Union soldier to death after she found him stealing a bridle from her barn! After this incident, the Union authorities told the Samuels they would have to leave the county. They moved to Rullo, Nebraska, although they still retained possession of their farm in Missouri. Major Rodgers had the young guerrilla carried to a steamboat and started him on the trip upriver so he could die in peace at home. Jesse reportedly met the soldier who shot him on the boat. They exchanged pictures and became friends; the soldier tended the young man gently on the cruise.

When Jesse reached his home in Rullo, Dr. Samuels told Zerelda there was little they could do for him. He lay near death for eight weeks. Zerelda said she often put her head to his chest to see if he was still alive, he was so pale. In his feverish state, Jesse begged his mother to take him home. "I don't want to be buried in a Northern state," he told her.

"We are going back to old Missouri if the trip kills every one of us," Zerelda finally told her family. "Jesse don't want to die here."

It took four men to carry the boy to the boat for the long journey home, a journey most of the family believed would end in death. Jesse lay unconscious most of the trip, according to his mother, waking only once to assure himself that they were really returning to Missouri. When the boat reached Kansas City, Jesse was carried to the boarding house owned by his uncle, John Mimms (married to Robert James' sister). This boarding house had been a meeting place for Kansas Jayhawkers and Redlegs during the war. Perhaps the family felt it was a safe place to harbor their son, since hostile feelings were still strong in the area.

They carried the critically ill guerrilla fighter into the boarding house. Waiting to nurse him was his twenty-year-old cousin, Zee Mimms. (Her name was also Zerelda, so to avoid confusion everyone called her Zee.) Zee was described as being small in build with fair hair and blue eyes. A friend of Jesse's called her "beautiful," while a news reporter remarked that she had an "intelligent-looking face." She had not seen her younger cousin in years, but there is no doubt she heard exciting tales of his exploits during the war. It was the perfect romantic situation. The pale, dying young man looking up from his bed of pain into the blue eyes of a lovely nurse. It is not surprising that the two young people fell in love that long summer.

Zee had a gentle, mild disposition that must have contrasted well with Jesse's excitable, erratic temperament. She nursed her cousin, assisted by his younger sister, Susie, and slowly Jesse's health improved. He was able to return to the farm in Kearney that fall, although still so weak they had to haul him in a wagon. Before he left, however, he and Zee were engaged to be married.

Chapter Seven

When the Shooting Stopped . . .

The war had ended, but hatred and bitterness were stirring in the brush. The Confederate flag still flew over the courthouse in Liberty, Missouri, only twelve miles from the James' farm. General Jo Shelby had become a hero to the Missourians as the only Confederate general never to surrender. Little Archie Clements was still roaming the countryside in the company of several other guerrillas, among them Dave Poole. The communities that had looked forward to a year of peace found more trouble on their hands with the return of the veterans.

Military rule was being relaxed in the communities, but civil authority was little more than a joke, as evidenced by the fact that the wild ex-guerrilla Dave Poole became sheriff of Lexington, Missouri. To make matters worse, radicals got control of the Missouri legislature and were determined that every rebel should pay for his allegiance to the lost cause. They passed an act providing amnesty for Union soldiers for acts of violence committed during the war, but this act did not include the guerrilla fighters or regular Confederate soldiers. This meant that anyone could accuse a Confederate soldier of murder in the death of a Union soldier killed in battle and could make the charge stand. The guerrillas, of course, were outlawed by regular laws of warfare.

The economy of the state and its people was creating problems too. Returning Confederate soldiers were impoverished. People who had all their savings in Confederate script were wiped out. General Order Number Eleven had turned many counties into wilderness. Families had lost homes, land, cattle, horses—all their worldly possessions. Farmland had been reclaimed by the brush. How were men to support their families? Money was needed to buy seed, clothing, and food. But the money was controlled by the banks, run by Yankees. They were unregulated and charged high interest rates, refused to loan money, and foreclosed on mortgages. Men were growing desperate.

Lawlessness was the result. Men who had known nothing but fighting and bloodshed since they were teenagers saw no reason to suffer when they could have what they wanted for the taking—and the taking was all the sweeter when they were taking from Yankees! Quantrill's ex-guerrillas were natural suspects. State law declared that a rebel had no legal rights. Missourians hadn't much use for judges or fair trials at the time anyhow. If a man was believed guilty by a majority of the citizens, they hanged him. Thus, to be arrested meant a short rope over the limb of a tall tree. Few boys hung around to see what the sheriff wanted when they heard his knock on the door.

The James family was no exception to hard times.

The neighbors remember that Frank, twenty-two years old in 1865, returned home following his surrender and stayed there to farm their land while his family was in Nebraska. Frank was a quiet man who mostly kept to himself. Following his strict Baptist upbringing, he apparently did not drink to excess and never ended up in rowdy barroom brawls. He was known to go around with guns strapped on, but that wasn't anything unusual. Most men and some women traveled armed in those unsettled days. If he associated with his old guerrilla friends, that was overlooked in Southern-sympathizing Clay County.

But the anger and hatred of the border days was still present. Frank claimed later that he was harassed by the authorities, and this could well be true. Radical Union officials had no intention of "easing up" on any of Quantrill's boys. Not everyone in Clay County was Southern, and the young man's life must have been difficult at times. Besides, plodding along behind the plow was boring work for the ex-guerrilla fighter. Farm life was grinding, unending, unrewarding in those hard times. The slaves were gone. Even when the family returned, Dr. Samuels was little help. He never fully recovered from his hanging experience. Jesse could barely get out of bed without assistance; his wound continued to drain. So most of the work fell to Frank and Zerelda and the older children, although Zerelda apparently hired a black woman to help with the cooking and housework.

Jesse continued to improve slowly. He had good days when he was up and about and bad days when the fever returned. He joined the Baptist church in Kearney and began singing in the choir. He attended church socials and parties on days he felt well enough, although one man recalled the time when Jesse walked out of a party looking pale. The man found his friend outdoors, draining his wound. When he finished, he calmly returned to the party. Jesse's favorite occupation was singing in the choir and he never missed a Sunday service if his health permitted. Frank, who never darkened the church door, had his father's books for relaxation. He continued to be a devoted student of Shakespeare and could quote long passages by memory. He also kept up with popular authors of the times.

Jesse's romance, unfortunately, was not blossoming. He had run into a large obstacle—his mother. Zerelda was violently opposed to her son's engagement. The Bible stated that first cousins were banned from marriage. Society did not condone first cousins marrying either. Zerelda was strongly religious and she refused to accept Jesse's choice. He faced another problem, too. He was his mother's favorite son and she was undoubtedly jealous of Zee. Zerelda ordered her son to end the engagement. But her son was strong-willed also. Although he was religious, he never let his religion stand in the way when he wanted something. As for society—he didn't give a hang about that. He told his mother he was going to marry Zee.

Like Frank, Jesse undoubtedly continued to meet with his old army buddies. Most of them were in the same sad economic condition, facing the Missouri winter with a scanty harvest and little or no money. When the boys got together to talk over old times, they must have remembered how easily Bloody Bill had robbed the banks in Union towns. Now Quantrill's boys needed money and it was in the hands of the old enemy. With this rationale what happened next should have come as no surprise to anyone.

Chapter Eight

The First Daylight Bank Robbery

Ten or twelve heavily armed men rode slowly into the town of Liberty, Missouri, on the afternoon of February 13, 1866. They attracted no particular attention. The townspeople were used to armed men roaming around. One or two of these men might have looked up at the rebel flag fluttering over the courthouse and smiled grimly.

Two of the men, dressed in Union overcoats, tied their horses outside the Clay County Savings Bank and sauntered inside. The other men posted themselves at various strategic locations around the bank. They had done this many times before during the war. This could have been any Kansas town.

Inside the bank, one man stopped by the stove to warm his hands. His companion walked over to the counter and asked the cashier's son, William Bird, to give him change for a bill. When William went to get the money, he found himself staring down the business end of a Colt revolver. He jumped back in terror. The robber leaped over the counter, his companion following, revolvers drawn. Greenup Bird, cashier, was ordered to put all the bank's money in a grain sack that one of the robbers carried. Bird was told not to make a sound or he would be shot. When William Bird didn't move quickly enough, he was struck in the back with a pistol and shoved into the vault. About $60,000 in gold, silver, government bonds, and paper currency went into the grain sack. The Birds were then ordered inside the vault. Greenup wanted to stop and discuss the matter, but was told he'd be a corpse if he didn't move. He moved. The bandits shut the vault door, but the lock didn't catch and the Birds were able to free themselves.

The two men ran from the bank, flung the grain sack over a horse, and jumped into their saddles while the townspeople watched in stunned amazement. Then the gang rode wildly out of town, firing their guns into the air and yipping the blood-chilling rebel yell. But not all the revolvers were fired harmlessly. A young student at William Jewell College—the college Robert James helped found—ran out into the street in excitement and was shot down and killed. He was not armed.

The young man's name was George Wymore, and the reason the outlaws shot him is not clear. Some bystanders say Wymore was yelling that the bank had been robbed and was trying to stop the bandits. But others said he just got in the way of a stray bullet. A curious legend tells that the Wymore family received a letter of condolence from Frank James, who stated that the boy was shot by accident. This letter was said to be in the possession of the Wymore family for years, but was lost or simply decayed through time, if it ever existed. Certainly it would have been unusual for Frank to implicate himself in the robbery at this time.

The citizens of Liberty immediately formed a posse which chased after the bandits until they crossed the river and disappeared into the brush. The posse returned, reporting that a snowstorm had wiped out the tracks. The town's banks got together and offered a $10,000 reward for capture of the men, but no one seemed interesting in collecting it, although at least six of the boys had been recognized. All six had ridden with Quantrill. Two of them, Don and Buddy Pence, were cousins of Frank and Jesse. Warrants were issued for three men, but only one was ever arrested and he was released when the prosecution failed to come up with a case. The money was never recovered.

There exists no concrete evidence that either Frank or Jesse was involved in the Liberty bank holdup. But the neighbors justifiably suspected Frank. Jesse claimed he was too weak to even mount a horse until the following spring, but that is open to doubt. None of the suspicions concerning the James boys was made public and, if the James' family's standard of living improved that winter, it was not commented upon openly. Not until the James boys became notorious outlaws would the Liberty bank job be attributed to them.

Five men rode into the town of Lexington, Missouri, on October 30, 1866 at noon. The place was quiet, most of the town's citizens were eating lunch. The bank cashier, J. R. Thomas, was busy with his books, when he looked up to see a customer approaching. The man asked Thomas if he could change a bill. The cashier agreed and opened the cash drawer to get the money. Then he became suspicious when two more "customers" strolled into the bank. He demanded to know who they were.

"Bank examiners," one of the young men replied with a grin and drew his revolver. He tossed over a grain sack with orders to fill it. The cashier put all the money from the cash drawer into the sack, but refused to open the vault. The robbers threatened to shoot him, but Thomas bravely stated that even if they shot him, they wouldn't find the key. The boys searched his pockets, then left hurriedly with only $2,000 in the grain sack—a long way from the $100,000 rumored to have been in the bank vault. Their horses were tied in an alley and the five men rode out of town quietly.

Thomas ran outside and raised the alarm. A posse was formed, headed by, of all people, Dave Poole. Naturally, the posse didn't catch their former comrades in arms, but Poole returned with an exciting story of how close they came. He said they actually spotted the bandits, but his horses just weren't fast enough to overtake the excellent steeds the outlaws were riding. The local paper reported the robbers were probably "Kansas redlegs!" No suspects were ever recognized (except maybe by Dave Poole), but the old-timers all state that nineteen-year-old Jesse James was "the bank examiner."

Chapter Nine

Jesse Turns Outlaw

All famous outlaws have a story to explain why they were driven to a life of crime. Robin Hood was caught shooting deer out of season and Quantrill was his "brother's" avenger. Jesse came up with his version, reported in stirring detail years later by Major John N. Edwards. Edwards was Jo Shelby's adjutant and became editor of a Kansas City newspaper after the war. He was a prolific writer, staunchly pro-Southern and never allowed facts to clutter up his romantic articles and books. He became the James' boys press agent and defender in later years and was primarily responsible for the creation of the popular myth that Jesse was an American Robin Hood.

The story Jesse told was printed by Edwards in 1873 as a series of articles titled "A Terrible Quintette." It is all unsubstantiated. Newspapers at the time would certainly have covered the story of the dramatic shoot-out. There is no mention of it anywhere. In the story, the soldiers came to arrest Jesse for refusing to surrender.

It is important to the understanding of the James' legend to remember that nearly everyone who read it believed it at the time. Some of the old guerrillas had met similar fates, including Little Archie Clements, who grinned his last on the streets of Lexington, shot down in ambush after a barroom brawl. It was because of widely circulated stories like this that the poor farmers and ex-Confederate soldiers, struggling to make ends meet, came to look upon Jesse and the boys as heroes—fighting the oppressive Yankee lawmen and striking out at cold-hearted Yankee bankers. Just as Quantrill and his men could not have survived without local help, the James brothers would become dependent upon their friends and neighbors who believed they stood for the lost cause.

According to Jesse, his old wound flared up during the winter of 1866 and he nearly died following a hemorrhage. Lying in bed, weak from fever and loss of blood, he heard a knock on the door. The date was February 18, 1867. Five soldiers outside demanded entry. Dr. Samuels went to Jesse's room and asked his stepson what he should do. Jesse told the doctor to help him reach the window. He looked out. The moon was full and reflected off the white snow. Jesse saw the soldiers' guns and knew for certain that these men were not here to swap old war stories. Jesse told his stepfather to stand clear. He strapped on his pistols. Then, barely able to walk, he crept downstairs.

The soldiers began hammering on the door with their rifles, calling for Jesse to come out or they would come in and take him—dead or alive. Jesse listened closely and put a revolver to the door. He fired and one of the soldiers fell with a howl. Then the ex-guerrilla fighter kicked the door open and blasted away with both revolvers. One of the soldiers fell dead and two others were wounded, but managed to ride off. The fifth escaped unharmed. Jesse James was now an outlaw. He left home the next day and went into hiding. Later that day an entire division of militia arrived to capture the boy who had reportedly never officially surrendered.

Jesse said he went to Kentucky, to be with Frank. But on March 2, 1867, the bank at Savannah, Missouri, near Kearney, was robbed in the same familiar pattern. Only this time, events took a startling turn for the bandits. Once again, the five armed men appeared riding into town at noon. Leaving one man to hold the horses, four of them entered the bank. At the sight of four strangers coming in during lunch hour, Judge John

McClain, the bank's owner, reacted quickly. He leaped up, slammed the door to the vault shut, and grabbed his gun. He began shooting at the robbers. The bandits, caught off guard, returned the fire and the judge fell. The judge's son watched in horror. Without thinking of his own danger, he dashed outside screaming, "Robbers! The bank is being robbed." The man holding the horses fired at the boy, but his horses reared in fright and it was all he could do to hold them.

The bandits ran out of the bank, caught their horses, and galloped out of town, the grain sack empty. A posse set out in pursuit, but returned several days later without success. Remembering what Quantrill had taught them—that a troop looking for a regiment will never find just one man—the robbers split up and rode off in five different directions. Judge McClain later recovered from his wound and came to be quite a hero to the townspeople. They would point him out in later years as the man "lucky" enough to have been shot by the famous Jesse James.

On May 22, 1867, the gang robbed the Richmond, Missouri, bank. Remembering their bitter defeat in Savannah, the boys decided to follow Quantrill's old attack plan for raiding towns. Richmond was peacefully conducting its business that spring day when twelve to fourteen men galloped into the city from all different directions, firing off their revolvers and screaming the rebel yell. Four of the men dismounted and dashed into the bank with the grain sack, demanding money. They got about $4,000. But if the border wars had toughened the guerrillas, it had also produced a civilian population that didn't frighten easily. Several citizens realized at once that their bank was the target. They began shooting at the outlaws. The bandits fired back. The mayor of Richmond was shot to death as he ran toward the bank with his pistol. A young man shooting at the bandits from behind a tree was struck in the head with a bullet and died instantly. Seeing his son fall, the father ran toward him and was also shot down. The robbers galloped out of town, but the fight in the streets gave a posse time to overtake them. After a brief skirmish, the men escaped and vanished into the brush.

Several of the boys were recognized. All were ex-Quantrill men. All were friends of Frank and Jesse. One, Allen Parmer, would later marry their sister, Susie. Allen came up with an alibi for this job, stating he was in St. Louis at the time, and provided several well-known, upstanding citizens as witnesses. But several of the others were arrested or attempts were made to arrest them. Payne Jones shot it out with sheriff's men at his father's home in Independence and escaped. The people of Richmond were furious. Two nights after the holdup, a mob dragged a man out of jail and hanged him from a tree outside of town. He had been safely in prison the whole time the robbery was committed, but it was rumored that he told a fellow inmate the day of the crime that the bank was going to be robbed. Another of Quantrill's men, Thomas Little, was being held for trial when he came up with an alibi for the day of the robbery. He, too, was lynched by a mob who feared a jury might not convict him. Almost a year later, two more of Quantrill's boys were recognized and apprehended in St. Louis, charged with the Richmond robbery. They were brought to Richmond to stand trial, but the citizens decided to skip the trial and move straight on to the execution. Missouri's reputation for ignoring legal formalities grew so bad that when another of Quantrill's boys was arrested in Kentucky, the Kentucky newspapers advised that any request to return the man to Missouri be denied.

In later years, when Missouri achieved a nationwide reputation as "the Outlaw State," the citizens would point to these lynchings and claim this proved that the people were really trying to establish law and order. Unfortunately, all it proved was that it was hard to tell the outlaws from the upstanding citizens. The men may have been guilty of robbery, but, because they died without a trial, all they could really be considered guilty of was having ridden with Quantrill. This was the way it was viewed by ex-guerrilla fighters and Confederate soldiers, who saw it as just another form of persecution. It also indicated that the state itself was one step removed from total anarchy. All of this would add to Jesse's story that he was driven into becoming an outlaw.

Chapter Ten

The Russellville Bank Robbery

Jesse James traveled to Kentucky in the summer of 1867. While on his way there, he may have stopped by the home of General Jo Shelby. Shelby had returned after his unsuccessful trip to Mexico, where he ended up on the losing side once more by fighting for Emperor Maxmillian. Shelby owned a farm just outside of Lexington, Missouri, and was always glad to welcome a former soldier, gray or blue, just as long as they could swap war stories. Quantrill's men were particularly welcome. Shelby never forgot the debt he owed them. Frank and Jesse both were frequent visitors.

On this particular day, however, when Jesse stopped by to see the General, his wife, Betsy, replied that her husband was not home. She invited the young man in for a visit, however, telling him to water his horse. They were walking toward the house, when a black youth employed by Shelby as a hired hand rushed up and begged Betsy to protect him. The young man had gotten into a fight with a white boy in town. It was, by all reports, a justified encounter, only the black youth made the mistake of defeating his opponent. Seeing that this might prove a costly victory, the black teenager took to his heels and ran all the way back to the farm, pursued by an angry mob ready to string him up. Mrs. Shelby was frantic. All she could do was hide her employee, but the mob might just take it into their heads to tear up the house looking for him.

Jesse offered to handle the situation. He knew the mob would have to cross a creek before they reached the Shelby farm, so he stationed himself on the bridge, his guns drawn. The mob approached, armed with picks, axes, and probably a rope. Jesse stood alone in the center of the bridge and told them that was as far as they were going. They looked at the sandy-haired young man with the rapidly blinking, cold blue eyes and suddenly decided the white boy had it coming. They backed up and hurriedly returned to town. Jesse assured Mrs. Shelby that the trouble was over and rode on his way, leaving the general with another debt of gratitude he owed the James brothers.

Jesse was in Tennessee when his wound began bothering him again. He went to a doctor in the summer of 1867 and was told the lung was badly decayed and death was near. (Much of Jesse's reckless disregard for his own life and his lack of respect for law and order may have stemmed from the fact that he believed he was dying.) He remained in Kentucky that summer. His relatives, the Hights, lived there, as did their cousins, Bud and Donny Pence. Jesse returned home in the fall. Zee Mimms was attending school at the Clay County Seminary in Liberty and Jesse visited her there, still going against his mother's wishes. The young men from William Jewell College were frequent visitors at the seminary also, and it is interesting to imagine Jesse fitting in with the well-educated college men. One local story tells that the seminary's spinster matron so frightened the daring young outlaw by her imperious manner that he had to leave in tongue-tied confusion.

Jesse left home once more and returned to Kentucky. His was a wandering, unsettled nature. There he met up with Frank and another of Quantrill's boys, Cole Younger. Cole had traveled to Texas following the war, where he fell under the spell of a Missouri girl named Myra Belle Shirley whose parents had been driven from Missouri for being Confederate spies. It is said that she and Cole had a daughter, but Cole wasn't about to settle down and neither was Myra Belle. He left for Missouri and his family's farm. Myra Belle "married" a horse thief first, and then a handsome Indian named Sam Starr. She began an outlaw career that the James boys might have envied under the name Belle Starr.

The boys stayed at a hotel in Chaplin, Kentucky, posing as cattle dealers. Their target was the bank at Russellville, where George Shepherd, another war buddy, lived. The boys entered the bank on March 20, 1868. Cole asked the banker to change a bill. The banker must not have cared for Cole's looks because he dropped the bill and headed for the nearest way out. One of the men fired at him, grazing his scalp. They dumped about $12,000 into the grain sack and rode out of town after exchanging shots with a few of the locals. No one else was hurt.

This time the bank wasn't satisfied with the posse's lame excuse that they'd lost the outlaws in the brush. They hired a detective, D. T. Bligh, who began an intensive investigation that eventually led straight to the two Missouri brothers lodged in the Chaplin Hotel. Unfortunately, Bligh came across the evidence that it was actually the James brothers involved in the robbery only after they'd become well-known criminals. All he could prove in 1868 was that the bandits came from and returned to Chaplin. Bligh later uncovered evidence that put Cole Younger at the Russellville holdup, along with George Shepherd and John Jarrette, who had been with Quantrill on his last ride. No arrests were made.

Jesse returned home in April. Although not under suspicion directly, it must have been nerve-racking for the young man to find a detective on his trail. A doctor in Kansas City advised Jesse to visit a warm and sunny climate to improve his health. This was welcome advice for the twenty-year-old restless outlaw, and he acted upon it at once. Money was, of course, no longer a problem. He decided to visit his uncle, Drury Woodson James, who was living in Paso Robles, California. Jesse traveled to New York, took a ship around the Cape Horn, landed at San Francisco, and traveled from there to his uncle's ranch. It is said that Jesse attempted to find his father's grave, but was unsuccessful. It is said he spent his time riding the range with the cowboys. His health improved, he returned home in the fall of 1868. Frank also came home that fall from Kentucky.

The boys hoped their wartime careers would be forgotten by now, according to Edwards, but Jesse related that he was continually harassed and plowed the fields "with three pistols strapped" to his belt. Both he and Frank apparently lived at home for a year without incident. No robberies are attributed to them during this time. Jesse was baptized into the Baptist church at Kearney and he continued singing in the choir. He was still "courting" Zee, but his mother made life increasingly difficult for the young people. Jesse was popular with the neighbors, despite his growing reputation as being "up to no good." Some said it was just a young man's usual wildness and figured he'd probably outgrow it.

Both brothers played with the younger children in the family. Susie was a grown woman now, nineteen years old. Their half-sister, Sallie, was ten. Johnnie Samuels was seven and Fannie Quantrill, named in honor of the dead guerrilla captain, was five. The baby of the family was Archie, who was two years old in 1868.

The horrible memories of the war were fading for most people, although the bitterness would never be totally erased from their lives. The Confederate flag still flew in Liberty. It would be two more years before it was finally lowered. Life was apparently going well for the James' family, although Jesse still claimed he was being harassed by the soldiers. Frank had his books and occasionally went out with some of the young ladies in the neighborhood, although he did not have a serious romance with any of them. The farm was prospering once again.

There is no doubt the boys could have settled down and become respected members of the community, as many of Quantrill's men were doing. Who can say what led them back on the outlaw trail, unless it was simply the lure of easy money and the craving for danger and excitement.

This time, however, their crime would brand them as murderers and thieves in the eyes of the law. The peaceful life was coming to an end forever for Frank and Jesse James.

Chapter Eleven

The Murder of Captain Sheets

Gallatin, Missouri, is a small town about forty miles north of Kearney. On December 7, 1869, Frank and Jesse rode into Gallatin and tied their horses outside of the Daviess County Savings Bank. Frank walked inside. He asked the cashier, Captain John Sheets, if he could change a $100 bill. Jesse entered and demanded a receipt for the exchange. Sheets sat down to write one out. Jesse studied the man intently, spoke a few words to Frank, and then took out his revolver. Coldly and without warning, Jesse shot Sheets to death with two bullets— one through the heart and one in the head. The captain was dead before he hit the floor.

The horrified bank clerk ran out of the bank screaming that Sheets had been murdered and the bank was being robbed. The boys fired at him as he fled, but only wounded him. He continued to yell and the townspeople started reaching for their guns. Jesse grabbed what money he could from the cash drawer and stuffed it into the grain sack. Frank called for him to hurry. He could see the citizens running toward the bank with their rifles. The two brothers ran outside and Frank jumped on his horse. Men began shooting at him. Frank returned their fire and galloped down the street. Then he realized Jesse was in trouble.

Jesse had followed Frank out of the bank, but his horse

plunged and bucked at the sound of the gunfire. Jesse's foot got tangled in the stirrup and the horse began dragging him down the streets of Gallatin while the enraged citizens took pot shots at him. Jesse finally broke loose, but the young outlaw's career might have ended violently in the dusty street if Frank had not returned under heavy fire, caught Jesse by the arm, and dragged him up behind on his own horse. They made it out of town safely and "borrowed" a horse from an unlucky farmer. Then they comfortably rode back to Clay County. They had only about $700 in the grain sack, but Jesse believed he had kept his vow to avenge a dead comrade. He thought he had killed Major Cox, the man responsible for the death of Bloody Bill Anderson.

A posse set out. As usual, they got nowhere. The bandits were traced into Clay County, but disappeared into the brush. Back in town, however, the people had the horse that had given Jesse such a bad few minutes. A fine animal anywhere within three counties was recognized and remembered. Frank and Jesse always rode the best horses available. Jesse's career as a robber is said to be nothing compared to his skill as a horse thief. The animal was identified within a week as belonging to Jesse James. If the James brothers had been merely suspected of being involved in previous Missouri holdups, the law had definite evidence now and they acted upon it without hesitation. The murderers of Captain Sheets were to be "shot down in their tracks," stated one local paper. For the first time, Frank and Jesse had a price on their heads. A $3,000 reward was offered for the capture of the bandits. The citizens of Gallatin set out to collect it and avenge the death of one of the town's leading men.

A posse rode to Clay County and presented evidence to the authorities. The deputy sheriff and his son accompanied the Gallatin men out to the James' farm to bring in the brothers. Several different accounts exist of what happened next. Probably the most accurate is the report in the local papers following the incident. No matter which account is related, however, it is obvious that the deputy and his men knew nothing about bringing in ex-guerrillas.

The deputy, John Thomason, had his men surround the James' home. They got off their horses and lay in wait for the brothers to appear, smugly believing they had not been observed. Everything was quiet on the farm. They watched in boredom while a black child, the son of the hired girl, ran out to play in the stable. But the child wasn't going to play in the stable. He went there with a message from Zerelda to her boys. The posse watched in amazement as the stable doors flew open. Frank and Jesse rode out, guns blazing. The startled deputy got off one shot, then grabbed his horse. The Gallatin men fired, but the James boys, on excellent horses, jumped the fence and galloped away through a field. The posse followed, but only the deputy's horse could take the fence and Thomason saw he was losing the race. He probably also had second thoughts about chasing after the two by himself. He dismounted to take better aim and fired. His horse took off in panic and raced after the outlaws. It even caught up with them and galloped next to the brothers for awhile, until Jesse shot it. Deputy Thomason had no choice but to return to the Samuel's farm and borrow a horse from Zerelda so he could get back to town. It is not difficult to imagine what advice the fiery Zerelda handed over with the horse.

This incident has an interesting sequel. Years later, Oscar Thomason, John's son, who had witnessed the escapade, was herding cattle in Texas. He and his men spotted two strangers. Thomason recognized them instantly. Unfortunately, the two also recognized him. They drew their guns.

"Are you looking for us?" one asked.

"No," replied Oscar thankfully, "we're not. We're hunting stray cattle."

"All right," Jesse replied and put his gun away. Then he and Frank invited the cowboys to share a meal with them. The men laughed and talked over old times.

"By the way," Jesse asked Oscar suddenly, "how much do you figure that horse of your father's was worth?"

"About fifty dollars, I guess," said Oscar.

Jesse fished out fifty dollars and handed it to the astonished Oscar. Then he and Frank packed their gear and rode off.

The governor of Missouri wired sheriffs in neighboring counties to be on the alert and the state militia was ordered to watch for the James Brothers. But Quantrill's boys knew every path, every trail, every cave and every out-of-the way church in western Missouri. They simply vanished. (Rural churches were excellent hiding places because no one ever went there during the week.)

One day, Kansas City newspaper readers were excited to read a letter from Jesse James himself. The Kansas City *Times* was edited by John Edwards, who let it be known that he admired the old guerrillas and joined in their fight for fair treatment after the war. This first letter from Jesse was to start a tradition of sending letters to the paper following each robbery. Jesse claimed he had not been in Gallatin the day of the robbery and was innocent of the murder of Captain Sheets. The reason he had run from the law officers was because he figured he'd never receive a fair trial. A few weeks later, another letter appeared giving alibis from important Kearney citizens claiming that Jesse was in their area only the day before the holdup. Letters from Zerelda, Dr. Samuels, and Jesse's sister Susie appeared in the paper, stating that the horse used in the robbery had been stolen only days earlier. They also said Jesse was home with them during the day of the robbery. Interestingly enough, no alibis were given for Frank's whereabouts.

It is doubtful whether the letters were really written by Jesse, who could barely write his own name according to those who knew him. Some claim they were written by Frank for Jesse or, more likely, Edwards, the romantic newspaperman wrote them. In any case, the letters had little effect except to bring Jesse's name to public attention. The murder of Captain Sheets started the brothers on the outlaw trail. There was no turning back.

Chapter Twelve

Something Wrong at the Bank

The James boys lay low for over a year following the Gallatin affair. Some say they went back to Kentucky, where their cousin Donny Pence had become a sheriff. But others claim the James brothers continued living at home, farming and riding unafraid around the countryside. Jesse had to quit singing in the choir, however. The elders in the Kearney church got together and read him out of the membership.

The summer of 1871 came to Missouri. The Confederate flag had finally been lowered from the Liberty courthouse. Jesse was twenty-three years old. Frank was twenty-eight. Most men their age had settled down and were raising families. But Jesse and Zee were still "keeping company," and Frank was not interested in getting tied down. On June 3, 1871, the bank in Corydon, Iowa was robbed by five men. Corydon was about 120 miles north of Kearney.

The Corydon bank holdup was probably one of the easiest robberies in history. A noted orator was in Corydon on that day, discussing the highly controversial issue of running the railroad through town. Feelings ran high and tempers had flared. It promised to be an interesting session. Nearly every one of the town's citizens went to the outdoor meeting, held on the church grounds outside of the city.

The five men rode into town and found the place deserted.

71

The businesses were locked and shuttered. The men, later identified as Frank and Jesse, Cole Younger, and another Quantrill man, Clell Miller, stared at one another in astonishment. (The other man with them was not identified.)

But, at least, the bank was open.

They walked in and tied up the cashier who was alone. Then they leisurely collected around $6,000 and walked out to the horses. The men trotted out of town, passing the meeting place on their way. The orator was in full voice, ranting and raving. Jesse rode up to the platform, edging his horse through the crowd.

"Excuse me," the outlaw interrupted, "but may I ask a question?"

"Well, what is it?" the famous orator snapped, annoyed at being interrupted in mid-thunder.

"Did you know there's something wrong at the bank?" Jesse asked. Then he and the gang rode off.

At first the crowd thought it was an attempt to harass the speaker and they shouted for him to continue. But a few men got nervous and decided they better take a look. They found the cashier bound and gagged, the money stolen. The speech broke up in a hurry. It was said that the next time Corydon, Iowa, held an outdoor meeting, the men all sat facing the bank.

The robbery had a major impact on the lives of the James brothers. For the first time, a bank called in the famous Pinkerton Detective Agency. This firm had a growing national reputation, primarily from work done during the Civil War. The detectives were not allowed to accept reward money, but were paid instead by the agency, which was based in Chicago. Robert Pinkerton, son of the founder, William Pinkerton, was sent to Iowa. He formed a posse of Corydon men and tracked the bandits back to Clay County. There he lost the trail, although it had been leading straight back to the James' farm. Robert Pinkerton is reported to have said later that the boys had so many friends and neighbors willing to lie for them that proving they were in on the bank robbery would be impossible. A private detective did manage to outwit Clell Miller, trapping him in a phoney horse-stealing plot. Miller was arrested, but his neighbors rushed to his defense and he was released when they swore he never left home.

The boys left Missouri again, probably returning to Kentucky. On April 29, 1872, the bank at Columbia, Kentucky, was robbed by five men. Their identity was never firmly established, but Detective Bligh was called in on the case and discovered that three men matching the descriptions of Frank, Jesse, and Cole Younger had been staying in the area, living with local families. Frank, in fact, became a great favorite with the family he stayed with. He borrowed a copy of *Pilgrim's Progress* from the elderly grandmother and read almost the entire book. A bookmark indicated the place where he set it down on the day of the robbery. The grandmother got quite indignant with the investigating officers, stating that such a kind, literate man could not be involved in a bank holdup.

The Columbia robbery was not the peaceful job the Corydon holdup had been. When the cashier was ordered to turn over the money, he foolishly began yelling "bank robbers" and was immediately shot dead. Two customers leaped from the windows and out into the street shouting for help. Another customer ran out the front door after a scuffle with one of the bandits. The boys grabbed what money they could and fled. A posse followed, but the gang used one of Quantrill's old tricks and circled around behind them, until the robbers were eventually following the confused posse. But the James gang had come out with only $600 and another dead man to account for. Detectives were tracking them relentlessly. The boys decided to head for home.

Frank did not get that far. He appeared at the home of his old friend General Jo Shelby one night, close to death. The general welcomed the outlaw and brought him inside without a moment's hesitation. He and his wife cared for Frank tenderly, bringing in doctors and sparing no expense. Soon the whole neighborhood knew the outlaw was staying with the Shelbys, but, of course, no one dared approach the feisty general with the suggestion that James be turned over to the authorities. Shelby told his friends that Frank was suffering from tuberculosis, but it was more likely a bullet in the lungs. Frank stayed with the Shelbys for two months, before he felt well enough to return home.

In September 1872, Kansas City held a great fair. People from miles around attended it and the James' boys were no exception. Three masked men walked up to the gates of the fairground, in broad daylight and in full view of a large crowd. They pulled their guns and demanded the contents of the cash box. The ticket seller tried to apprehend the robber, who had just dumped about $900 into the grain sack, but one of the other gunmen fired a shot at the ticket taker, who released his hold. The trio raced away while the crowd watched in thrilled excitement. The only injury was a small child who received a flesh wound from the spent bullet.

Rumors spread that the daring holdup was the work of Frank and Jesse. Some accounts even say Jesse told his name to the ticket taker while he was demanding the money. Major Edwards published an editorial that criticized the crime, but asked the public to admire the daring and bravery of the robbers who had the nerve to commit a robbery in the midst of such a large crowd. A rival newspaper, however, suggested that there were no others in existence more deserving of being hanged after endangering the lives of hundreds of innocent people and actually injuring a small child.

A letter appeared in the paper, signed Jesse James, protesting his innocence. Another letter was published by Edwards which began to establish the Robin Hood image of the brothers. Although this letter was not signed, it stated that the robbers considered themselves more honest than the crooked politicians running the state who stole millions from poor people. The outlaws stated they only killed in self-defense, apologized for wounding the child, and offered to pay the medical bills. They ended by swearing that they only stole from the rich to give to the poor. (Who these poor were, other than themselves, is not known.)

The bank at St. Genevieve, Missouri, was robbed on May 27, 1873, and once again the James boys were suspected. Two men entered the bank, cleaned out nearly $4,000, and then forced the cashier to accompany them outside, using him as a shield. Two more men held the horses and the gang galloped off after stealing the cashier's watch. Unfortunately, one of the horses threw his rider and ran off down the road, the grain sack filled with money tied to its saddle. The bandits stared after it gloomily. Then a farmer driving a wagon happened along. The robbers waved a gun in his direction and ordered him to catch the horse. He did so and they rode off.

But bank robbery was beginning to lose its charm. It was turning into a lot of hard work with uncertain rewards and the distinct possibility that the bandits might be shot down by irate citizens. Another prospect came into view and the boys were quick to take advantage of it.

Chapter Thirteen

"Go Chase 'Em Yerself"

If Gallup had been around polling people in the 1870s, the reputation for being the most hated corporation in America would have been won hands down by the railroads. Graft and corruption were widespread in the industry that was growing by miles of new track daily. Speculators were watering railroad stock and investors lost thousands of dollars in the Railroad Panic of 1873. Farmers were being charged exorbitant rates for freight shipments and, if they protested, the railroads shut them out. States began forming railroad commissions in an attempt to handle the situation, and finally a federal agency was organized in 1875 to control the industry. Before that, however, the James boys decided to strike their own profitable blow at the system.

The James gang was not the first to rob trains, as some have claimed. This dubious distinction is held by the Reno brothers, who robbed a train in Indiana in 1866. The fact that the Renos were captured and three of them hanged did not stop Frank and Jesse from pursuing this new outlaw career with enthusiasm. It promised to be much more profitable than bank robbery.

The James boys, Cole Younger and his little brother, Jim, plus several more unidentified men headed north out of Missouri in July 1873. They split up. Frank and Cole traveled to Omaha, Nebraska, where gold shipments from the west were passing through that town on the Chicago, Rock Island & Pacific line. Frank and Cole were supposed to determine which train was carrying the gold and pass this information on to Jesse. He and his boys planned to meet the train as it came through Iowa.

On the night of July 25, five men broke into a handcar shed near Council Bluffs, Iowa, stealing hammers and a spike-bar. With this equipment they pried loose a section of rail and pulled it out of line at a point where the train would slow for a curve. They believed that this would simply force the train to come to a stop. It did. Unfortunately, the train not only stopped, it turned over. The engineer, John Rafferty, was crushed to death. Cars derailed and people were thrown from their seats, although no one else was seriously injured.

Startled by this unexpected event, the robbers were nevertheless capable of handling the chaotic situation. They opened the express safe, expecting to see thousands in gold. But Frank and Cole had slipped up. The gold shipment had come through only a few hours earlier. All the gang got for their trouble was about $2,000. They ordered the passengers out of the coaches and made them drop their valuables into the grain sack. Then the gang rode off, waving their hats in the air and shouting friendly farewells, while the passengers gathered around the broken body of the dead man and wondered what to do next.

The robbers all wore masks, but later descriptions matched those of the James and the Youngers. Scraps of conversation overheard between the men indicated that twenty-five-year-old Jesse was the leader, giving commands to the rest who obeyed him without hesitation. The railroad crew immediately went to the local farmers to get up a posse, but the response was disappointing.

"It ain't my money they stole. Go chase 'em yerself."

It is said that when a posse finally was formed, it turned around and headed for home as soon as the men began to suspect whom they were following. The trail led directly to Clay County.

But the railroads didn't give up. This wasn't some small-town bank Jesse'd robbed. It was a giant corporation. He had killed an engineer, upset wealthy passengers, and stolen company money. The railroads immediately hired the Pinkertons and offered a $5,000 reward. The state of Iowa kicked in $600.

A newspaper in St. Louis, where John Edwards was now working, received a letter from Jesse in December 1873, denying his part in the robbery. The letter came from the Montana territory, so apparently the pursuit was getting a little too close for comfort and the boys headed out west to let things cool off. Jesse offered to turn himself in, and Frank, too, if they could be assured of a fair trial and guaranteed protection from mobs and the governor of Iowa. Jesse also stated, however, that he and Frank would never be taken alive, but would be glad of a trial to have "this long and sleepless vigilance on our part broken up."

When the governor didn't respond, the gang tried robbing a stagecoach in Arkansas, but this proved less profitable. They did add a new dimension to the legend, however, when Cole Younger told any man who had served in the Confederate army to step forward. One man did so and the bandits immediately returned his money and jewelry, shaking his hand and stating that they only robbed Yankees. This tale was widely repeated and much appreciated by the pro-Southerners, who used it to show the boys still believed in the lost cause. In reality, this was the only known time the gang ever mixed business with politics.

The James gang, as they were now being called, returned to Missouri and announced their arrival by holding up a train at Gads Hill. Frank might have chosen this location for a holdup as a joke. Gads Hill is the scene of a famous robbery from the Shakespearean play *Henry IV*. In the play, bumbling Sir John Falstaff is duped into robbing a group of travelers by Prince Hal and his friend. Sir John is then robbed in turn by the disguised prince, who gets much merriment listening to the old liar's account of the heroics he performed during the robbery.

Frank carried a volume of Shakespeare with him in his saddle-bags and often read it to pass the time before a robbery, much to the disgust of the other men in the gang. It must have amused him to rob a group of travelers at Gads Hill, just like old Falstaff, but it is interesting to wonder if he tried explaining the joke to the other boys.

In fact, the entire Gads Hill robbery turned into something of a joke from beginning to end and became a standard part of the James-Younger legend. No one was killed or even injured. The boys captured the station agent and his friends in the station house. The train was due in at 5:40 P.M. They hoisted a signal flag outside, which indicated to the engineer that he was to stop and pick up a passenger. The train stopped and the "passengers" all boarded, using guns instead of tickets. They took an undetermined amount of money from the express company safe, some reports say it was as much as $20,000.

Then they robbed the passengers. But, like the stage robbery, this had a unique twist. One of the men (perhaps Cole Younger) ordered the travelers to hold out their hands for inspection. The outlaws examined each person's hands carefully. If the hands were rough and work-hardened, no money was taken from that person. But any man or woman with smooth, white hands was assumed to be wealthy and was instantly ordered to make a contribution to the grain sack. One man, suspected of being a Pinkerton agent, was taken into a room and strip-searched, but the robbers let him go. Finally Jesse handed a crewman a written account of the holdup, including a blank space to fill in the amount of money taken. This was to be given to reporters.

The gang galloped off, heading west, into the sunset. No one was in a tearing hurry to chase after them, but a reluctant posse gathered the next morning and followed in half-hearted pursuit. Reports began coming in from across the state that the outlaws were stopping here and there, staying with farmers and paying handsomely for their meals. It was a traditional part of Western hospitality for families to offer food and shelter to traveling strangers. No payment was expected, generally. The stranger was supposed to pay for his meal by relating any news, helping to pass the long evenings. But these strangers paid for their meals in gold, sometimes leaving a farmer more than he could earn in a year's work. Before they left each morning, the leader would lift his hat and announce, "You might be interested to know that I am Jesse James."

This naturally impressed the farmers and became the source for many tales that were passed down to future generations. Even today, there are Missourians who tell about the time Jesse ate dinner with great-grandpappy, leaving a gold piece on the table when he left.

But the governor of Missouri was not amused. He offered a $2,000 reward for the "bodies of the robbers." The railroad put increased pressure on the detectives and the Pinkertons began closing in.

Chapter Fourteen

The Pinkertons and the Bridegrooms

The famous detective agency was now strongly committed to capturing the James and Younger brothers, who had successfully evaded the law for at least nine years. They put their best men on the track of the brothers. But the suave Eastern detectives were no match for the ex-guerrilla fighters who had outwitted Union generals with ease. Pinkerton's men made the mistake of thinking they were chasing chicken-stealing farm boys, instead of cold, calculating criminals. The agency paid for its mistakes, but never did learn from them.

In March 1874, shortly after the Gads Hill robbery, a young man named John Whicher arrived in Liberty. He was only twenty-six years old, but had already made a name for himself in the Pinkerton organization. The capture of the James' brothers singlehandedly would be a glittering accomplishment. Whicher went to the bank president in Liberty and announced that he was going to bring in Frank and Jesse. The president told him he was crazy, but Whicher had a plan. He was going to disguise himself as a worthless drifter and get hired as a farm laborer at the James' home. He revealed the same plan to the Liberty sheriff. Both men told the young detective he was a blithering idiot to imagine such a simpleminded plan would fool the boys. The sheriff even told him that Zerelda herself would kill him, if her sons didn't. But Whicher refused to listen to reason.

Whicher disguised himself in rough working clothes and boarded a train to Kearney. People saw him get off the train and head down the road toward the Samuels' farm. Late that night, a ferry operator took four men across the Missouri River. One was bound and gagged. The three told the ferryman that they had captured a horse thief and were bringing him to justice. Descriptions of the young men matched Jesse James, Jim Anderson, and another Quantrill man, Arthur McCoy. The bound and gagged "horse thief" matched the description of John Whicher.

The young detective's body was found near Independence, on the other side of the river from Kearney. He had been shot twice in the heart and the head.

Several days later, two Pinkerton men appeared in St. Clair County on the trail of the Youngers. Their names were Louis Lull and John Boyle. Lull was from Chicago and Boyle was a Missouri man out of St. Louis. They picked up deputy sheriff Edwin Daniel and started out for the Younger home. (What the three of them hoped to accomplish against the four desperate brothers is not clear.) On their way they stopped at the house of an old man, said to be a friend of the Youngers. They asked for directions to the house. The old man told them and they rode off.

But watching from a window were John and Jim Younger, who just happened to be eating there. They grew suspicious and followed the three. Pulling their guns, the Youngers ordered the men to halt. Being an old Missouri boy, Boyle knew the game was up and immediately headed off into the brush. The other two men dropped their weapons. Lull, realizing his life was worthless if the boys found out who they were, pulled a small pistol from his hip pocket and fired, hitting John Younger in the neck. The detective put the spurs to his horse, but John managed to fire his shotgun at Lull before he (John) fell

Independence Academy, George Bryant, teacher. The future Mrs. Frank James is the fourth from left, center, second row.

from his saddle. Daniels tried to escape in the excitement, but Jim Younger shot him down. Jim went to help his brother, but John was beyond help—the first of the notorious gang to die. Lull escaped, but he died six weeks later.

Daniels died that day. Jim escaped uninjured.

That violent spring seemed like an odd time for Jesse to be thinking romantic thoughts, but he and Zee decided to get married that April. They had been keeping company for nine years. Jesse was twenty-seven and Zee was twenty-nine. Zee's mother had been as much opposed to the match as Jesse's and had tried to persuade her daughter to find a more sedate boyfriend, but Zee's devotion to Jesse never wavered. When her mother died, other relatives took up the argument against marrying an outlaw, but finally her sister agreed to let Zee be married in her house. The date for the wedding was April 24, 1874. An uncle, Reverend William James, reluctantly agreed to perform the ceremony.

It must have been an interesting wedding. The groom appeared suddenly out of nowhere, armed and carefully on the alert for any strange faces among the friends and relatives gathered for the occasion. When Jesse entered the house, he was collared by the irate preacher-uncle, who proceeded to berate the young man for his evil ways. Then he tried to talk Zee out of marrying a man with a reward on his head. Jesse said he was innocent, he was being persecuted by the law officers. The argument dragged on and several men in the crowd began to get nervous. They weren't used to staying in one place for such a long time. Finally the Reverend James, in an ill-humor, married the two that evening. They left that night for Texas.

Romance entered quiet Frank's life about the same time. He had met a young Independence schoolteacher named Annie Ralston while crossing a creek one day. The water was running high and Annie couldn't reach her home without making a long detour. Frank happened to be passing and gallantly offered to take the lady across on his horse. He began to call on Annie regularly, under another name, of course. Her father, Colonel Samuel Ralston, was a highly respected Independence

Annie Ralston James, Samuel Ralston, Jr., Margaret Ralston, and Harry Ralston

citizen. Frank eventually told Annie who he really was, but it apparently made no difference to the twenty-two-year-old young woman for she agreed to marry him. She did not, however, have courage enough to tell her family about her bridegroom. She packed her bags and left her home "to visit relatives," but soon after, probably in June 1874, her mother received this note, "Dear Mother, I am married and going West." Months later the stunned Ralstons would find out accidentally the name of the man their daughter had married.

Frank, thirty-two, and Annie were believed married in Omaha, Nebraska, and traveled from there to spend their honeymoon with Jesse and Zee at the home of their sister, Susie James Parmer, in Texas. Various robberies and holdups that occurred at this time in Texas were credited to the James gang, but they are impossible to verify. One incident does sound like Jesse's sense of humor, however. A minister was forced to turn over a beautiful gold watch to a band of masked outlaws. When he protested that they should not steal from a man of the cloth, one of the boys told him he didn't need a watch—Christ never carried one. But the gang's notoriety was such that any time a man was robbed, he swore the James brothers were responsible. They were even accused of robberies occurring in different states on the same day.

This made it more difficult than ever for the Pinkertons to keep on their trail. But they did.

Chapter Fifteen

Fire in the Night

The audacity of the James and Younger brothers in their daring daylight robberies, plus the inability of the local authorities to bring them to justice, gave both the outlaws and the state of Missouri much national attention. The attention was not favorable. Elected officials were accused of condoning banditry. These charges grew so serious that the James brothers became a political issue threatening the status of the then present administration. Missouri governor Silas Woodson offered more reward money for their capture and was vocal in denouncing the outlaws. Politicians argued for bringing them to justice in the campaigns of 1874. John Edwards began running special sections in the St. Louis paper relating the lives of the brothers in romantic detail. He told of their bravery in fighting with the guerrillas and gave a heart-rending account of the hanging of Dr. Samuels. He denied the guilt of the boys in any robbery attributed to them, but applauded the daring of the bold highwaymen. People read these stories avidly, and they added to the controversy over whether the boys were common thieves or noble Robin Hoods.

The James boys returned to Missouri in August 1874 and celebrated by holding up a stagecoach outside of Lexington. This robbery was committed on a Sunday afternoon in full view of a number of people out for a walk after dinner. It proved to be the highlight of the day. Three men with guns ran out from behind a house and ordered the stage driver to stop.

They held their guns on him and told the passengers to step outside. Eight men and one woman climbed out, raising their hands in the air.

Word of the holdup spread quickly and people gathered to watch. The leader of the gang ordered one of his men to prevent the onlookers from spreading the alarm, but one daring young woman broke away and ran to the ferry operator, explaining what was taking place. He took his boat across the river yelling that the stage was being robbed. This caused an enthusiastic crowd to gather on the opposite bank as well. Suddenly one of the women in the crowd recognized friends. Mattie Hamlet called out a greeting to Frank and Jesse. Frank returned the greeting and they fell into a discussion. She begged him to give back the money and jewelry they'd stolen from three of the passengers who were friends of hers, and Frank readily handed the people their valuables. Mattie remarked that stagecoach robbing seemed a bit of a comedown for the notorious gang and Frank agreed. Finally the robbers galloped off with their loot to the delight of the admiring crowd.

The newspapers were full of the robbery and everyone seemed to have enjoyed it very much, including those being robbed. One man on the stage that day said he was pleased that he had been held up by men of "such national reputation." The Lexington papers came out with a special edition that stated, among other things, "they [the James-Youngers] have bourne themselves like men who have only to die, and are determined to do it without flinching . . . [they have] defied the whole power of Missouri. They have laughed at her Governor . . . [they are] brilliant, bold, indefatigable roughriders." It is no wonder James and Frank soon began to believe themselves to be heroes.

But the state of Missouri was not laughing. The Governor and detectives were beginning to look like fools and they went grimly about their task of catching the outlaws. A detective reported that he had engaged James and Frank in a running gun battle that fall. He believed he hit Jesse, but his posse could not catch them. He complained that they never stayed in one place long enough.

What were Zee and Annie doing during this time? Did they follow their outlaw husbands from one hideout to another, always riding at night, staying hidden indoors during the day, starting up in alarm at the sound of horses hooves? Did Zee open the door to her husband one night to find him covered with blood after a battle with detectives? No one knows. The lives of these two women are forever buried in the shadows.

Another train was robbed in December at Muncie, Kansas. Five men on splendid horses captured the depot and forced the men inside to lay railroad ties across the track. When the train stopped, the robbers ordered the engineer to uncouple the passenger cars and pull the baggage and express cars forward. They took about $30,000 and then watched with interest as the crew hitched the cars back up. Reports started drifting in that Jesse and one of the Younger boys had been seen hanging around Kansas City a few days before the robbery. A week later, a friend of the James brothers, Bud McDaniel, was arrested. He was one of the first gang members who was not a former guerrilla. A large sum of money and some of the jewelry taken in the robbery was found in his possession. But he refused to betray his accomplices. More reward money was offered, but few people thought about collecting it.

The railroads put more pressure on the Pinkertons. Why couldn't the sophisticated agency catch a couple of Missouri farm boys? On the night of January 26, 1875, the Pinkertons tried, but with tragic results.

That night, a special train left Kansas City in deepest secrecy. It was carrying nine men. The train headed for Kearney, but did not stop at the depot. It continued to a point about three miles farther, near the James' farm. The men climbed out

Dr. and Mrs. Zerelda James Samuels at home in Kearney, Missouri. "X"s mark Dr. and Mrs. Samuels.

and began walking down the road in the darkness. As they passed a neighboring farm, a man came out of the brush and joined them. He was a hired hand on the farm of Daniel Askew, a man named Jack Ladd. The men crept up to the house in the pitch blackness of the night and encircled it. They found two horses in the stable that showed every sign of having been recently ridden. They believed Frank and Jesse were inside. But fourteen-year-old Johnnie and twelve-year-old Fannie had been to a party at a nearby farm. The horses were theirs.

The Samuels were sleeping when they heard a noise outdoors. They rushed to the kitchen and found what they thought was a bomb, hissing and smoking on the floor. Dr. and Mrs. Samuels attempted to shovel the thing into the fireplace. Nine-year-old Archie wandered in to see what all the excitement was about. Their black servant, Chloe, and her son, Ambrose, had been asleep in the kitchen. They watched as Dr. Samuels got the thing into the glowing coals, where suddenly the device exploded.

A fragment tore into the side of the little boy. He fell to the

Original wing, James home, Kearney, Missouri. "X" over window marks spot where Pinkerton agents threw bomb that resulted in Mrs. Samuels loosing her arm.

floor, screaming and bleeding. Zerelda's right hand, holding the fireplace shovel, was so severely injured in the blast that it was hanging in shreds. Dr. Samuels amputated his wife's hand and stopped the bleeding, but there was nothing he could do for his son. Archie died within an hour. Chloe was injured in the blast, too, but not seriously.

One of the older children ran to the neighbors for help. The men outside apparently fled at the unexpected explosion, although some reports indicate that the James brothers were there at the time and began firing at them. Ambrose also grabbed a gun and shot at the dark shadows running into the night. That morning a gun was found outside. The initials "P.G.G." were stamped on the handle. Those initials stood for Pinkerton Government Guard and were found on the handle of every Pinkerton man's weapon. The hired man, Jack Ladd, disappeared. It was soon common knowledge that he was a Pinkerton agent in disguise. It was believed that he died of gunshot wounds that night. The nine men were said to have carried the body of a tenth off the train with them when it returned to Kansas City.

Newspapers across Missouri angrily tore into the Pinkertons, accusing them of blacker crimes than Frank or Jesse had ever committed. After all, neither of them had murdered a child or harmed a woman. Public outcry was so loud that the governor was forced to start an investigation of the bombing. A Clay County grand jury indicted Allan Pinkerton, among others, for the murder of little Archie Samuels. Nothing came of it, however. Local legend says that hot-tempered Jesse traveled to Chicago with the intention of shooting Pinkerton, but he was never able to get a clean shot at the man and so was forced to abandon the attempt.

The Pinkerton side of the story is somewhat different. They claimed that their men surrounded the house and called for Zerelda and Dr. Samuels to open the door and let them in. The Samuels refused. The house was dark and the detectives could not see who was inside so they tossed in a device designed to light up a room. It was a round metal ball filled with kerosene with a wick in it. The agency claimed that their incendiary device would not have exploded if the Samuels had left it alone, but contact with the fireplace coals caused the gas inside to expand and explode.

George Caleb Bingham. Best known for his career as an artist, he investigated the bombing of the James home at Kearney by Pinkerton agents.

One unanswered question concerns the whereabouts of the brothers. Were they really at home? A local doctor, who was called in after the explosion, said that Zerelda locked herself in a room to tell someone good-bye. The doctor never saw this person, but when he was ready to leave, he went outside and found his horse missing. It was mysteriously returned several days later, muddy and exhausted.

The only thing the raid on the James' farm accomplished was to brand the detectives as murderers of children. Public sympathy was on the side of the outlaws.

The boys were beginning to believe their own legends.

They were beginning to believe they were invincible.

Chapter Sixteen

Disaster at Northfield, Minnesota

Public outrage over the bombing led to a bill in the Missouri legislature to grant amnesty to the James boys and Youngers for their Civil War crimes. It failed, but only by a narrow margin. Whether the boys would have really "come in" if the bill passed is doubtful. Only three months after the bombing, in April 1875, their neighbor, Daniel Askew, was shot dead on his doorstep. Askew was suspected of having been in on the ill-fated raid, since the Pinkerton agent, Jack Ladd, had worked for him. Some say Jesse shot him out of revenge, but an interesting rumor floated out of Chicago—Askew had supposedly threatened to reveal what he knew about the raid and the Pinkertons decided to shut him up.

Letters from Jesse continued to appear in the papers. He enjoyed seeing his name in print. They proclaimed his innocence, thanked Confederate friends for their support, and threatened death to the Pinkertons. One interesting letter is a prayer from Jesse calling upon God to deliver Pinkerton into his hands. This strengthened the belief that Jesse was in Chicago gunning for the detective, but the brothers were also seen in Kentucky that summer. Jesse had a reason to stay home in August, wherever home was. His first son, Jesse Edwards James, was born on August 31, 1875.

But he wasn't home long. The bank at Huntington, West

Virginia, was robbed in the fall of 1875. One of the gang was killed and at first it was reported to be Jesse, but it was Thompson McDaniel, brother of Bud, who had been arrested following the train robbery at Muncie. Neither Frank nor Cole was positively identified, but both were suspected as well as Jesse. The gang came away with $10,000. This was apparently enough to see them through the harsh Missouri winter, for no robberies are attributed to them until May 1876, when a series of stagecoach holdups in Texas led the press to announce the brothers were back in action. Legend says Belle Starr was one of the gang when they were in Texas.

The train at Otterville, Missouri, was robbed in July 1876 by a group of men whose descriptions matched the James brothers and the Youngers. Maybe they were celebrating the country's centennial in their own unique fashion. The newspapers praised the coolness and daring of the bandits and reported that no great harm was done since the express company was the only one who lost any money. They were out $15,000. A minister led the passengers in prayer during the holdup and everyone sang hymns, which Jesse must have enjoyed. Pursuit of the bandits was half-hearted, and the posse was vastly relieved when they failed to catch sight of the criminals. No one wanted to get killed over express company money.

The quiet town of Independence was shocked when twelve detectives swept down on the home of respected Colonel Ralston one day in August 1876. The searched the house, but found no one there of a suspicious nature. The well-kept secret was out, however, and the colonel was forced to admit publicly that his daughter was Frank James' wife. Newspapers reported that Frank had been at the home only months before and got into a violent quarrel with Colonel Ralston, who demanded to see his daughter. Frank told him he couldn't, that Annie was far away. Having an outlaw for a son-in-law and being forced to submit to detective searches must have been a heartbreaking experience for the Ralstons, but they apparently never failed to support either their daughter or her husband when he was in trouble.

It wasn't detectives, but a Missouri lawman who finally captured a member of the notorious gang. Hobbs Kerry was identified by a farmer as having been near Otterville the day before the robbery with a party of men whose descriptions matched the James boys and the Younger brothers. Kerry confessed that he had robbed the train. He stated that Jesse, Frank, Cole and Bob Younger, Clell Miller, Charlie Pitts, and Bill Chadwell were all involved. The usual letters of denial came from Jesse and from Zerelda, too. Many people believed them, but their faith in Jesse as an innocent victim of wartime persecution was being shaken. It would crumble completely as the boys left Missouri that summer, heading north to what would become one of the most famous bank robberies in the history of the United States.

Eight men rode into the town of Northfield, Minnesota, on September 7, 1876. The men did not ride in together. Jesse, Bob Younger, and Charlie Pitts rode in first and hitched their horses to a rack outside of the First National Bank. It is said that Charlie and Bob had been drinking heavily, against

Bob Younger, who died in prison.

John Younger,
shot to death by
Pinkerton agents.

Jesse's orders. The men crossed the street. They were dressed
in the long white linen dusters often worn by cattlemen to protect their clothes from the dirt. The dusters also came in handy
to hide revolvers. The three sat down on some boxes and
watched the people walking up and down the street. Soon Cole
and Clell Miller came riding into town. Cole developed trouble
with his saddle right in front of the bank. He got off his horse
to fix it, standing in the middle of the street so he could see in
both directions. Jesse and his men slowly got up and strolled
into the bank. Clell quickly followed, pulling the bank door
shut behind him. Clell had also been drinking.

Clell stood guard by the door. He could see Cole outside,
still fiddling with his saddle. Jesse walked up to the teller's
window, guns drawn. One of the bookkeepers fell to his knees
and began to pray. The bandits ignored him and asked for the
cashier, but that fortunate man was on vacation. The assistant
cashier, Joseph Lee Heywood, was in charge. Jesse told
Heywood to open the safe. He replied that he couldn't, it had a

time lock. This was true, but the safe door was usually left open during the day, just a crack, for the convenience of the bank employees. It was open that day. Charlie Pitts entered the vault to have a look at the safe. Heywood leaped forward to shut the door on Charlie and trap him, an extremely foolish move with three other armed men in the bank. Jesse and Bob pulled the cashier back, insisting that he open the safe. He refused and they struck him over the head with a revolver. Heywood fell to the floor, bleeding. The boys were in trouble. The perfect timing needed to pull off the job was gone.

Suddenly Clell Miller got into an argument at the door with a customer who was trying to enter the bank. When Clell refused to let him in, the man guessed immediately what was happening and rushed away yelling for help. Cole jumped on his horse and drew his guns. A man in the bank took advantage of the confusion to crash through the back door. Charlie Pitts fired after him, wounding him, but he still got away. The citizens began arming themselves. Two hardware dealers

James Younger, who committed suicide.

Coleman Younger, who lived to tell his story that crime didn't pay.

grabbed guns and ammunition from their display cases and began firing at Cole. A young college student took one of his father's guns, ran upstairs to a second-story window, and shot at the men in the street. Cole was still trying to keep people away from the bank and returning the fire of the citizens.

Frank, Jim Younger, and Bill Chadwell galloped into town firing their revolvers and yelling. They shot down a Swedish immigrant who did not understand English and therefore did not obey the robbers when they told him to get off the street. The boys were being riddled with gunfire from the citizens, and those people who could not get guns began throwing rocks at the outlaws. Seeing that Cole and Frank were in trouble, Clell Miller ran to join them.

Jesse, Bob, and Charlie heard the gunfire. Suddenly one of the men outside yelled for them to hurry. "They're killing our boys!" In bitter anger and frustration, Jesse shot and killed the helpless Heywood, who was trying to pull himself up off the floor. Some claim Jesse slit Heywood's throat first, in the style of the late, unlamented Little Archie Clements. Jesse and the others ran outside, empty-handed, to a nightmarish scene. Bill

Chadwell and Clell Miller lay dead in the street. Cole was bleeding from a shoulder wound, Frank had been hit in the leg, and Jim Younger had blood pouring out of his mouth. Jesse mounted and rode off after Frank. Cole followed them, but stopped when he heard Bob call for help. He had been shot in the arm, shattering his elbow. His horse, which he had been trying to get on, was killed. Bob cooly shifted his gun from his right hand to his left and continued firing. Cole came back after his wounded brother. With bullets zinging all around them, he dragged Bob up on his horse.

The boys probably figured the worst was over when they were safely out of town. They expected the usual ineffective posse would most certainly turn back when they found out who they were chasing. But this wasn't Missouri. The citizens of Northfield didn't care who these men were. They'd killed innocent people. They were going to pay.

Chapter Seventeen

Pursuit, Capture, and Death

The boys were in desperate trouble. Jesse was the only one not wounded. They were in unfamiliar territory. Bill Chadwell, whose real name was Bill Stiles, had been going to lead them out of Minnesota. But Bill's body was in the Northfield morgue being photographed. They were a long way from the friendly Missouri brush and, what was worse, a long way from Missouri friends to shelter and care for them. Word of the robbery had been flashed by telegraph to every town in Minnesota. In no time, any man who could get a gun was out, eager to capture the robbers and earn a reward.

As soon as they bound the bleeding bullet wounds, the first order of business for the outlaws was to find Bob Younger a horse. Cole was six feet tall and heavily built. One horse had all it could do to carry him without adding his brother's weight. The boys stole several horses, but something went wrong with each. This delayed them. They headed for a swamp where they believed they could lose their pursuers. Unfortunately, their pursuers headed for the same swamp.

Riding through the bog proved impossible. The gang left their horses tied in what they believed was a safe place and started on foot. They ran into their first piece of luck—an abandoned house. They took stock of the situation. It was grim. Bob Younger, the most seriously injured, was getting worse. He was in terrible pain, was feverish, and infection was setting in. All of the injured men were weak from loss of blood. Food supplies were low and they did not dare shoot anything, fearing the posse would hear the shots. They stayed in the cabin as long as possible, then set out again, only to find that their horses had broken away. The animals were discovered by a jubilant posse who realized they were chasing men who were on foot. Four days after the robbery, a posse spotted the boys. They had only managed to get fifteen miles away from North-field. After a minor skirmish, they escaped again.

As Quantrill had counseled, in a tight spot, split up. This seemed the most logical thing to do, but according to Cole Younger, there was more to the band separating than a desire to confuse the posse. According to Cole, Jesse wanted to either shoot Bob Younger or leave him behind. The seriously wounded young man was slowing them up. A bitter argument followed among the men who had been friends for so long. Cole told the James boys he would never leave his brother and said they could clear out if they wanted to. Some accounts say Jesse blamed the failure of the holdup on Bob and Charlie's drinking. Whatever the reason, the gang split up. Frank and Jesse went in one direction, the Youngers another. Charlie Pitts stayed with the Youngers.

The first thing Jesse decided to do was steal two horses. Frank was limping from his leg wound. They came across a farm during the night and took two horses out of the barnyard in the darkness. They had only ridden a short distance when Frank's horse began to stumble about and act strangely. He discovered that the horse was blind. Jesse's horse turned out to be blind in one eye. The brothers abandoned their worthless mounts and set out again on foot. It is estimated that between two hundred and nine hundred Minnesota men were on their trail. The pursuit had grown so large, in fact, that a former Civil War general was called in to organize things so the posses didn't end up shooting one another. The boys had only one thing in their favor—none of the lawmen had a picture of either of them. They headed on toward Missouri.

The Youngers and Charlie Pitts struggled off in the opposite direction. They stopped at a farmhouse and begged for food, claiming they were hunters and had been injured in an accident. But a seventeen-year-old farm boy figured out who they were and dashed off after help. Pursuit was swift, when the boy finally convinced the authorities to believe him. The town of Madelia, Minnesota, gathered a posse together and headed out after the men. The Youngers and Charlie, unfamiliar with the territory, wound up trapped in another swamp.

The lawmen easily picked up their trail and soon saw their men. They called out for the boys to surrender, but the Youngers fired at them and stumbled on. The posse returned the fire. Charlie Pitts dropped dead, hit by five bullets. Cole and Jim and Bob Younger crouched in the swamp, wondering if they should fight it out. But they had been hit again in the shooting. Cole Younger reportedly had eleven bullet wounds when he was captured. It was either surrender or die face down in the mud. Bob Younger stood up, bleeding from another wound in the breast, his arm in a bloody, dirt-covered sling. He raised his good hand in surrender.

The Youngers figured they'd be promptly hanged from the nearest tree, but the men in the posse treated them kindly. They put Charlie's body in a wagon and assisted the brothers into town where their wounds were dressed and they were clothed and given food and water. Minnesota law provided that anyone confessing to a crime would receive life imprisonment instead of hanging. The Youngers confessed without delay. Once in jail, Cole gave his life story to a jailhouse audience of reporters and reduced several of the men to tears when he described his father's murder and his mother's mistreatment at the hands of Union soldiers.

The James brothers stole two more horses and reached the outer line of guards surrounding the area. They galloped through the lines and escaped, although Jesse was hit in the thigh. No one knows the details of their trip through Minnesota except that they rode hard, stealing fresh horses when they could. Legend says they told anyone who questioned them that they were lawmen in pursuit of the James-Younger gang who had robbed the bank at Northfield. Several people recalled meeting the two on their journey. They described Frank as being polite and reserved. But Jesse was gloomy and refused to talk, unusual for the fun-loving, sociable young man. Maybe he was remembering other men—William Quantrill, Bloody Bill, Little Archie Clements—who led such charmed lives and died such terrible deaths.

Chapter Eighteen

Mr. Woodson
and Mr. Howard

The brothers finally reached Missouri, where they were reunited with their families and had their wounds treated. But they knew that this time they couldn't stay in their home state. The arrest of the Youngers and the deaths of the other Missouri boys had shaken the faith of people who thought the James boys had been unjustly accused of crimes all these years. Detectives had been watching Jackson County closely, although they apparently did not suspect that Zee and her little son were living in Kansas City under an assumed name. (Jesse, Jr. had so many aliases during his childhood, it is said that he did not even know his real name or his father's real name until after Jesse's death.) The outlaws had no trouble slipping into town.

The detectives had only vague descriptions of the men. There were no photographs available. One Pinkerton detective who had been on the trail of Cole Younger for six years traveled to Minnesota just to see what he looked like. Legend says Jesse met Detective Bligh once and even ate lunch with him. Bligh did not recognize the man he had spent years tracking down and told the stranger he'd like to have one look at Jesse James before he died. Jesse later sent Bligh a letter saying, "You've seen Jesse James. Now you can go ahead and die."

But the brothers knew it was only a matter of time before they heard the ominous knock on the door, so they packed up their families and their possessions in covered wagons and drove across Missouri into Tennessee. They split up—Jesse stopping at the town of Waverly in August 1877, while Frank traveled on to Nashville. They there lived undisturbed until 1879. The brothers apparently saw little of one another during their stay in Tennessee. This may have been a precautionary measure or there may have been bad feelings between the two. Some say Frank was upset over the way Jesse had treated the Youngers.

Mr. J. D. Howard, as Jesse was known to his neighbors, wasn't much of a farmer. He was, however, generally well liked. He made friends easily, joined the local church, and started singing in the choir again. He had an eye for horseflesh and owned a very remarkable horse called Red Fox, which he raced at every opportunity. The neighbors said he was an extraordinarily good rider and won most of his races.

Financially, things went from bad to worse for the Howards. Farming was a lot of work for little reward, especially if a man is used to making money very quickly. By 1878, Jesse was borrowing money to live on from friends. One man recalled loaning Mr. Howard $60. Finally, the farm experiment was given up. Jesse decided he might be happier raising cattle. He acquired some stock worth about $900 from a man named Cooley. Jesse promised to pay Cooley when he was able to. But the hot-tempered young man and Cooley disagreed in a short time and Cooley demanded his money. Jesse refused, packed up his family, and moved out of town without leaving a forwarding address. He did repay the $60 he owed his friend first.

The James family left behind two tiny graves, dug in back of the house. Jesse carved the little headstones by hand. Zee had given birth to twins, but the infants died within a week. Jesse, Zee, and Jesse, Jr. showed up on Frank's doorstep in 1879. Jesse was destitute.

Frank, alias B. J. Woodson, had settled down and was enjoying life in Nashville, after he regained his health which had been impaired by wandering around in the swamps of North-field. He got a good job hauling wood for a lumber company. The only odd thing his employer remembered noticing about Mr. Woodson was that he always had a horse saddled and ready to ride near where he worked. He and Annie rented a house. Their neighbors said they were a quiet, hard-working couple who always paid the rent on time. Frank eventually made enough money to rent a farm, which he worked along with his lumber-hauling. He made friends with the sheriff of Davidson County and a circuit court judge. Frank raised hogs and even won a prize for them at the county fair. He, too, was fond of horse racing and often acted as starter for the races. Later he bought a racehorse himself.

Life was looking good for Frank, and there is every reason to believe that he was planning to settle down. His son, Robert Franklin, was born in 1878. Like little Jesse, the child was given an alias, but Frank even went one step further. Legend says he disguised the baby as a girl, calling the child "Mary." If anyone came looking for Frank James who had a son, all they'd find would be Mr. Woodson with a daughter.

When Jesse arrived on his doorstep, Frank was not over-whelmed with joy at seeing his brother.

Chapter Nineteen

The Glendale
Train Robbery

Jesse lived with Frank for several months, helping with the farming. Zee even nursed little Robbie when Annie found she could not nurse her baby herself. Jesse joined the local church and began singing once more. But he was restless and frustrated. He left his family in Frank's care and headed west, traveling to New Mexico to look things over. He stayed with an old school mate who ran a hotel in Las Vegas.

Jesse's daughter, Mary, was born July 1879, in Frank James' home. Jesse was thirty-one years old now, hardly a wild young man anymore. But he had a family to provide for. Farming was not appealing. Neither were the long hours of work Frank put in. Jesse decided to return to the career that he knew best. He was going back to Missouri.

Frank argued against it, telling Jesse he'd only put their family's lives in danger again. He urged Jesse to stay and give up the wild life, but the man was as head-strong and willful as the boy had been. Jesse ignored his brother's advice and rode back home to Kearney. Once there, he put the word out. Jesse James was back and needed men. He got them. Ed Miller, brother to Clell who had died at Northfield; Wood Hite, a cousin and former Quantrill man; Tucker Bassham, whose father and uncles had ridden with Quantrill; Bill Ryan; and a twenty-seven-year-old man named Dick Liddil, who would later turn traitor.

Dick met Jesse at the home of a former guerrilla, Bob Hudspeth, near Independence, probably right before the Glendale robbery. Jesse invited the young man to join them. Liddil agreed, although he didn't even own a gun at the time. Jesse told his new gang he was planning to rob the Chicago and Alton train at the little town of Glendale, not far from Independence. The boys made their plans, then separated. Liddil went to Kansas City to buy a set of Smith and Wesson revolvers from a pawn shop. Jesse went to spend a few days with his friend Jo Shelby. The men met on October 8, 1879, and rode into Glendale at sunset.

Bassham, Ryan, and Liddil walked into Joe Matt's general store. It wasn't much of a store, containing "cigars, plug tobacco, and a few canned goods." The real attraction was a barrel of whiskey in the back with a faucet and a tin cup on a handle. According to one fourteen-year-old, "All you had to do was give Joe a dime, walk back and wait on yourself . . . while Joe looked the other way." The presence of the whiskey barrel probably accounted for the fact that the entire male population of Glendale was in Joe Matt's store that night, about twelve to fifteen men. The bandits told them the party was over, they were invited to a train robbing. The men were herded down to the depot at gunpoint where Jesse, Ed Miller, and Wood Hite waited.

James ordered the stationmaster not to touch the telegraph equipment and then he proceeded to tear it up. Tucker Bassham mistook it for a sewing machine and tried to stop Jesse from destroying it, to the general amusement of all the hostages. Two of the gang placed railroad ties across the tracks, then everyone stood around waiting for the train. The group in the depot soon began talking quietly. Jesse asked them to be quiet occasionally, so he could hear the train whistle, but otherwise he left them alone. One of the young boys lit up a corncob pipe and Jesse asked to borrow it. He stood smoking the pipe, watching out the window. The train's light came in sight.

The robbers ordered the stationmaster to flag the train to a stop. At first he refused, but one of the men stuck a revolver in his mouth and he changed his mind. When the train came to a halt, Dick Liddil ran out to the engine with his new guns and ordered the fireman and engineer to raise their hands. Bill Ryan tried to uncouple the express car from the passenger coaches, but a patent coupling device defeated him so he went back to the passenger cars. Wood Hite and Tucker Bassham held their guns on the people, ordering them to stay in the cars and keep away from the windows. Jesse and Ed Miller beat on the door of the express car, but the messenger refused to open it.

They fired a few shots into the air to frighten him and Jesse shot a few times at a man with a lantern at the rear of the train, apparently not hitting him. Miller got a sledgehammer and began beating in the door. Finally the express man opened up. He had been trying to shovel the contents of the safe into a bag, hoping to jump for it when the door opened. But Jesse struck him over the head with his revolver and grabbed the bag from his hand. Then he walked up to the engineer and said, "I didn't get your name, but mine is Jesse James." The robbers rode off. They gave the rebel yell as they disappeared into the brush. The gang escaped with nearly $6,000, although early accounts placed the amount nearer $50,000. None of the bandits wore masks, according to the witnesses. But they were bearded and had their hats pulled low over their faces. One witness estimated the entire job took less than twenty-five minutes.

The passengers were not robbed in the Glendale holdup, an unusual circumstance. According to Dick Liddil, someone fired a shot from the passenger car that went through Wood Hite's "drawers and pants." Jesse said that since they were being fired upon they better leave. No other accounts contain the story of the bullet, but in the confusion and excitement of the robbery the passengers and the train crew may not have noticed.

The gang split up and divided the loot, each one getting over

$1,000 each. Jesse went back to Nashville with money in his saddlebags and an exciting tale for Frank. Jesse's sun was shining brightly again. The long tedious days of honest living were over. He had money and his name was back in the newspapers. But the shadows were beginning to lengthen for the desperado, although he did not notice them at the time. It all started with the arrest of Tucker Bassham, who attracted suspicion in his neighborhood of Cracker's Neck, near Independence, by spending money everyone knew he was too dumb to have earned honestly. He was arrested in July 1880, and charged with the Glendale holdup. Bassham pleaded guilty and was sentenced to ten years in the state penitentiary. Tucker himself was no great loss to the gang, and Jesse probably gave his arrest little thought.

But the sun was setting.

Chapter Twenty

The Capture of Bill Ryan

Jesse returned to Nashville, but he was not home much, being constantly in and out on "private business." He had moved his family out of Frank's house. He sometimes returned to his mother's, meeting Dick Liddil, Bill Ryan, and the Hites, Wood and his brother Clarence.

A story told by Jesse, Jr. may have happened around this time and relates the narrowest escape Jesse ever had from the law. He and a companion were riding through the brush one hot summer day, suffering from the heat and thirst, when they came upon the Little Blue River, clear and cool. The men looked at each other. Then they jumped off their horses, led the animals to the water, and, while the horses were drinking, the outlaws took off their clothes and dove in. They were splashing and shouting, up to their necks in the river, when a man appeared on the banks holding a shotgun.

"I know who you are. Put up your hands!" he called, standing between the outlaws, their clothes, and their guns.

The men had no choice. Slowly they raised their hands. This is said to be the only time Jesse James ever put up his hands at anyone's command and it is the only time he was ever captured.

There was no time to form a plan, but the boys were used to surprises and quick thinking. Jesse walked slowly toward the man, his hands in the air, arguing and protesting. He and his friend were having a quiet dip. Why were they being disturbed? He climbed out of the water, onto the bank, still talking. His companion remained in the water as if paralyzed by fright. When Jesse was within a few feet of the man with the gun, his friend suddenly let out a shrill war yell and dove into the water. This startled the man with the gun. He turned and Jesse had him.

All was over within moments. The man stated he was chasing two local horse thieves and mistook the boys for them. He apologized for disturbing them and Jesse ducked him in the river to teach him a lesson about annoying "honest men." The outlaws rode in one direction and their captor another, never dreaming what fame and fortune had almost been his. It is said that Jesse James never went for a swim again, no matter how hot the day or how inviting the water.

Various robberies occurred in the area of Missouri, Kentucky, and Tennessee at this time which are attributed to Jesse, but he is not known to have been involved in any until the robbery of a stagecoach near Mammoth Cave in Kentucky on September 3, 1880. Bill Ryan and Dick Liddil had come for a visit with Jesse. He took them to see Frank one Sunday, but Frank wasn't interested in joining the gang. He was still working and satisfied with his honest way of life. He disliked Jesse and Ryan hanging around, fearing it might implicate him in whatever they were up to. So the boys rode off without Frank, intending to rob the stage. Everything was planned, but a violent rainstorm drenched the outlaws waiting in the woods and forced the gang to change the date. Liddil left Jesse and Ryan, who told him "they would knock around the county and see what they could rob." They decided to try the stage again on a dry day.

The stagecoach with seven passengers was rattling along when two masked men stopped it and ordered the driver to raise his hands. The passengers were invited to step out and hand over their valuables. A wealthy, well-known Kentucky judge was aboard the stage along with his daughter. The judge dropped a beautiful and valuable gold watch into the grain sack; it had been a present from the governor of the state. His daughter handed over, among other jewelry, a diamond ring with her nickname carved inside the band. While Jesse held the passengers at gunpoint, Bill Ryan pulled out a bottle and drank to their health. Then they galloped off. The two divided up the take, around $800 cash value. Jesse admired the watch and the diamond ring. He kept both. He gave the ring to Zee, who had it resized to fit her finger. (So much for the story that Zee didn't know what her husband did for a living.) The watch was found among Jesse's possessions after his death. Bill Ryan got a silver watch which he later pawned for a saddle. Jesse gave another watch to Dick Liddil.

No one knows what lured Frank back to the outlaw trail. Maybe Jesse's stories brought back all the old excitement and the lust for easy money. He joined the boys in a series of smaller robberies, described by Dick Liddil, which took place during the winter of 1880–81. These little jobs didn't amount to much, however. One netted the daring bandits $4.23 plus a watch. The gang decided to go after bigger game and planned to rob the paymaster at Muscle Shoals, Alabama. Liddil claimed that Frank, Jesse, and Bill Ryan stole $5,000 from the man. Liddil said he wasn't involved in the robbery.

According to Dick, Jesse tried to get him to help murder Jim Cummins, a former guerrilla rider and gang member who may have been involved as early as the Liberty robbery. Jesse feared the weak Cummins would betray them and wanted him out of the way. This was apparently the beginning of Jesse's paranoid fear of traitors in the gang. The reward money was a tremendous lure. Dick refused, however, and, since disagreeing with Jesse was not a healthy occupation, he left town rapidly. So did Jim Cummins.

As it turned out, it wasn't Cummins who betrayed the gang,

but Bill Ryan and his whiskey bottle. On March 26, 1881, Bill wandered into a bar on the outskirts of Nashville and demanded whiskey and oysters. Bill suddenly turned nasty, drew his revolver, and ordered people "to stand back and give him room." Then he announced in a loud voice that he was "Tom Hill the outlaw" and offered to fight anyone in the bar, threatening to fill them with holes. This statement sobered up the bar crowd and one of them ran outside to find help. A detective named Weatherend happened to be passing by. Returning to the bar with the customer, Weatherend captured the drunken Ryan with help from the crowd. They found $1,300 on him and hauled him off to jail where he must have awakened with the worst hangover of his life. Descriptions of "Tom Hill the outlaw" went out to police officials around the country. Kansas City fired back, "We think he is Bill Ryan of Jackson County." Soon Ryan was on his way to Missouri, charged with the robbery of the Chicago and Alton train in Glendale.

Ryan's arrest came as a terrible blow to Frank and Jesse.

The three of them had been seen together in Nashville. Ryan was known to have even lived for a time with both brothers. Jesse's wife broke the news to him when he returned home that evening. He met Frank that night and the two decided they must leave town. The brothers rode out the next day, leaving their wives and children to handle the business of packing up. Liddil turned up again. He and Jesse settled their differences, and Liddil rode with Jesse to Kentucky. Frank met them there at the home of their cousins, the Hites. Jesse set about forming a new gang, making plans to return to Missouri.

Ryan's arrest had not shaken them much after all.

Chapter Twenty-One

Murder on the C.R.I. and P.

Jesse and Dick returned to Missouri in April 1881. Clarence Hite escorted Zee and her children back to Kansas City where they stayed at the home of a friend. Clarence rode to Mrs. Samuels'. There he met Frank and his brother Wood as well as Dick and Jesse. The men made plans to hold up the train at Winston, Missouri, in June.

The gang left for Winston, stopping at various farms along the way for a meal or to spend the night. They reached the planned location of the holdup and hid to wait for the train's arrival. But train robbing has its hardships like most jobs. While hiding in the woods, a Missouri rain soaked the outlaws, leaving them, according to Clarence Hite, "wringing wet." To make matters worse, poor Jesse "caught the toothache . . . and his face swelled up so he could hardly see." They took the suffering outlaw to the home of a man who lived near the tracks, stayed the night, and paid him to drive Jesse to the station the next morning. The robbery was postponed.

A week later Jesse felt better. He sent a message to his brother, Johnnie Samuels, to bring his horse to him. The robbery was back on. The boys rode down to the area around Winston again, stopping once more at different houses in the area until they got near the town itself. Then they slept in the woods and fields, leaving two of the gang on guard duty. They intended to rob the train at Cameron, but too many people got on and they left. Then they planned to rob the train at Gallatin, but hitched their horses too far away and the train passed unmolested. They finally returned to Winston.

Some of the gang must have believed this robbery was under an evil star, but they went ahead with it as planned. Things continued to go wrong. The bandits used a different approach this time. Instead of stopping the train, they got on board, posing as cattle dealers once again, dressed in their long, white linen dusters. When the train got outside of town, Clarence and Dick climbed over the coal car to the engine. They fired their guns several times at the engineer and firemen to scare them into stopping the train. The train came to a halt. Both Dick and Clarence heard gunfire back in the passenger cars where Frank, Jesse, and Wood Hite were riding.

According to the newspaper accounts, the conductor, William Westfall, was passing through the car collecting tickets when Jesse stood up behind him and ordered him to raise his hands. Westfall went for his gun and Jesse fired, hitting the conductor with a shotgun blast in the back. Westfall staggered toward the rear of the car and Jesse shot him a second time. The man's body fell off the train. Jesse proceeded to the express car, which he entered through the rear door. Frank and Wood tried to get in through the side door, but the baggageman was standing in the doorway trying to see what was going on. Frank grabbed the man by the leg and pulled him out the door, hurling him to the ground. Unfortunately the baggageman took Wood Hite with him, dragging him off the train in his fall. As they hit the ground, Frank jumped into the express car, then either he or Jesse yelled for Dick and Clarence to force the engineer to start the train.

The train gathered speed, leaving Wood Hite behind, along with the body of the murdered conductor. The baggageman was able to jump back on. Frank and Jesse kept firing into the passenger car, supposedly without intending to hurt anyone. But bullets were flying all around the car, and the passengers were trying desperately to hide under their seats. One young man, a stone mason named Frank MacMillan, was crouched on the platform of the passenger car when he heard a voice that he thought was his father's calling for help. He jumped up and looked in the window. He was struck in the head with a bullet and dropped off the train. Frank James would later be charged with MacMillan's murder. Meanwhile he and Jesse ordered the expressman to open the safe with his key, which the man did. He handed out all the bundles of money. Jesse asked if that was all. The agent assured him it was. Jesse told him he had killed the conductor. The agent was next. The man pleaded for his life. Jesse cruelly ordered him to drop to his knees. The agent refused and Jesse struck him over the head with his revolver. Then he and the others jumped from the moving train, about one quarter of a mile from where their horses were tied. The passengers were not robbed.

But all the James gang got for this trouble was $800.

Public outcry was loud over the Winston robbery, the Glendale robbery, and the murders of Westfall and MacMillan. There were still those who came to Jesse's defense, however, with the story that Westfall had been the conductor on the train that carried the Pinkerton agents to the James' farm the night of the fire-bombing. Westfall may have been the conductor, but Jesse did not know that at the time he killed him. According to Clarence, Jesse said he was sorry he had killed the conductor right after the robbery, but the man had reached for a gun and Jesse shot him in self-defense. After the stories about Westfall appeared in the papers, Jesse said he was glad he'd shot him—he had it coming.

Whatever Jesse's reasons, the public was no longer interested. They were tired of violence. The romantic legend was fading.

Chapter Twenty-Two

The Trial of Bill Ryan

Two men vowed in 1880 that they would break the James gang and bring the boys to justice. These men were not after reward money. They were not bold Pinkerton detectives, fast-drawing sheriffs, or evil-eyed bounty hunters. No legends or songs have been written about them, yet they were responsible for the downfall of the most famous outlaws in American history. One was a prosecuting attorney in Jackson County and the other was the governor of Missouri. Both were motivated by political ambition.

Following his election, Thomas Crittenden, governor of Missouri, stated publicly that he would rid the state of the bandits who were giving it the name of "The Outlaw's Paradise." Missourians shook their heads, they'd heard this before. But, following the Winston robbery, Crittenden met with officials of the railroads and offered $5,000 for the capture of the James brothers and an additional $5,000 for the murderers of Captain Sheets and William Westfall. This was an unusual act for a governor and many people criticized Crittenden for being in kahoots with the railroads. Most people considered the railroad companies to be bigger crooks than Frank and Jesse. But Crittenden stuck to his guns. He had to have bait money and he couldn't get it from the legislature. He was convinced the only way to catch the outlaws was to entice one of the band into turning traitor.

The prosecuting attorney was a fascinating man named William Wallace. A Bible-pounding lawyer, Wallace campaigned

William H. Wallace, prosecuting attorney who did more than all the Pinkertons put together to break up the notorious outlaw gang.

in Jackson County on the platform that he would never rest until the James gang was destroyed. It was a dangerous platform and one for which he very nearly got shot. Wallace received threats against his life even while he was campaigning, but he won. His first real test came with the arrest of Bill Ryan. He knew that if Ryan was found guilty, it was the beginning of the end for the gang. He exerted all his efforts and his resources toward this end. His associates told him he was crazy—no Missouri jury would ever find one of the famous gang guilty.

Ryan came to trial in September 1881. It was held in the Jackson County courthouse located in Independence in the heart of James' country. There was more excitement in the town than at any time since the war. Hundreds of Ryan's friends and supporters rode in, all of them armed and threatening trouble. Friends of the James brothers were there, too. Frank and Jesse were reported to be in the area, and it was rumored that they would try and rescue their old gang member. Wallace received so many threats against his life that he never left home or his office without a revolver in his coat. His friends told him they expected to see him shot down at any moment.

Wallace instructed the Chicago and Alton railroad companies to send their men who were on the Glendale train down to testify. At first the company refused, saying that this would only anger the James gang and cause Jesse to rob their trains exclusively. Wallace insisted, threatening legal action, and the men finally arrived. But when they saw the blood-thirsty mob gathered in Independence, the railroad men begged Wallace to release them from testifying, swearing that if he put them on the stand they would say nothing. Having been fairly certain that this would happen, Wallace agreed, using only the testimony of the express messenger who had been knocked unconscious to prove that a robbery had taken place. Wallace had a surprise witness, if he could only keep him alive.

The crowd in the courthouse was so large that there was

Jackson County Court House, Independence, Missouri. Wallace brought Ryan to trial here and thus began to break the power of the James gang. (This is the fourth remodeling of the building.)

hardly room to breathe, let alone move around. Men slept in the streets so they could get a seat when the doors opened every morning. Bill Ryan was being defended by the best legal counsel in Missouri, including a former congressman from the area. No doubt the defense felt elated when the railroad men refused to take the stand, but their elation evaporated quickly when Wallace called Tucker Bassham to testify. The attorneys protested vehemently. Bassham was a convicted criminal and under Missouri law could not testify. In full view of the astounded crowd, Wallace handed Bassham a pardon signed by the governor.

Although Wallace must have had doubts about his client's intelligence, Bassham proved to be an excellent witness, sticking to his story stubbornly in the heat of cross-examination. He described the Glendale robbery in detail. The jury, all local men, listened to the testimony attentively. They retired and came back with a decision that stunned the entire state. Bill Ryan was found guilty of train robbery. The judge sentenced him to twenty-five years in prison. The courthouse crowd exploded in fury, and the jurors rode back to their homes in fear of their lives. One man lived only half a mile from Ryan's parents. Tempers cooled, however, and no one was hurt, although a mob burned Tucker's home to the ground. Bassham himself fled a short time after the trial. Wallace allowed him to go, stating that he would call him to testify if the James brothers were captured. The attorney even took Bassham's picture for the purpose of identifying him later. But Tucker vanished and was never seen again.

Wallace was jubilant over the Ryan decision. Now he was certain it was just a matter of time for the James boys; the noose was drawing in around their necks. But Frank and Jesse weren't caught yet. In a bold act of defiance, the brothers robbed the Chicago and Alton train at Blue Cut (near Glendale) right in the midst of the Ryan trial.

Chapter Twenty-Three

The Last Holdup

The robbery of the Chicago and Alton train at Blue Cut during the Ryan trial clearly showed Jesse's attitude. Dick Liddil confessed later that the gang tried to figure out a way to rescue Ryan when he was caught. But the attempt was given up. The boys never believed the jury would find Ryan guilty anyway.

Jesse was living quietly in Kansas City that fall with his wife and children. He had an alias, as did the rest of the family, and he only went out at night. Groceries were delivered to the home and Zee never visited the neighbors. Frank stayed with the Ralston's for a short time, although Annie and son Robbie were not with him. Relations were strained between the brothers. Liddil testified that Jesse had objected to Annie's returning to this part of the country, apparently because she had been talking too much. Frank sent her to General Shelby's where, it was later revealed, she attempted to get in touch with Governor Crittenden to arrange for Frank's surrender. When that effort failed, she left Missouri on Frank's orders. Jesse was becoming more paranoid all the time. Frank might have figured his life was worthless if Jesse ever found out he was considering turning himself in.

Jesse had killed Ed Miller that spring, suspecting Ed of turning against the gang. According to Clarence Hite, Ed and Jesse got into an argument over some tobacco. Jesse may have deliberately goaded the man into the fight. Ed waited until

Jesse's back was turned and then fired a shot at him that whistled through Jesse's hat. It was a fatal miss for Ed Miller. Jesse turned and "shot him off his horse."

Jesse sent out word that a robbery was being planned and the gang gathered. The boys used a series of code letters, delivered to various "safe" homes, then taken by messenger to the outlaws. Johnnie Samuels was a messenger, as were other area boys. The gang was made up of Wood and Clarence Hite, and Charlie Ford, a new member whose sister, Martha Bolton, was a friend of Dick Liddil's. The boys stayed at the Bolton house frequently. Dick Liddil, Frank, and Jesse completed the band. They made two attempts to rob trains before the date of the seventh, but one train ran over a piece of iron placed on the track to stop it and another robbery was given up "because we were very tired," according to Dick. The real reason may have been that a large number of armed men were seen riding on the platform. So the boys chose the Chicago and Alton train that ran through Blue Cut on September 7. It was reportedly carrying $100,000.

The boys met in the brush near the railroad on September 5, Jesse's thirty-fourth birthday. The next day they crept to within a few hundred yards of the Ralston home, where Frank left them and brought back food in a basket. They traveled to Glendale, riding at night, and hid in the brush during the day. Dick rode into town for food, returning with "bread and raw meat." Train robbing was not easy, comfortable work, but the nights are still warm in Missouri in early September and life for the old Quantrill guerrillas in the brush was probably not too tough.

When night fell, the men piled rocks across the track and devised a red signal to stop the train by tying a piece of red flannel around a lantern. Wood Hite and Charlie were put in charge of stopping the train and capturing the engineer. They were then supposed to rob the express car. Jesse and Frank were to stand on one side of the track and keep the passengers in the cars while Dick and Clarence took the other side.

The plan started off smoothly. The train stopped in response to the red signal and everyone except Jesse boarded with guns drawn. They forced the fireman to break open the door to the express car with a sledgehammer, but after several blows, the messenger opened it from inside. Wood and Charlie jumped into the car and leveled their revolvers at the messenger, who had tried to hide in the rear of the car. They asked him for the key to the safe. He said he did not have it. They threatened him and the man suddenly found his key. He opened the safe. Charlie and Wood took out the few bundles of money inside and reported to Jesse that they'd apparently hit the wrong train. Jesse suggested robbing the passengers then, to make their night's work worthwhile. Charlie angrily knocked the messenger over the head a few times, accusing him of hiding the loot. The man collapsed on the floor, bleeding and unconscious.

While this was going on in the baggage car, the conductor suddenly realized that a freight train was due to come along in a few minutes and would crash into the passenger train unless someone stopped it. He ordered his brakeman to grab a lantern and flag down the oncoming train. Brakeman Burton ran down the tracks, waving his lantern. The outlaws didn't realize what he was doing and began firing at him. Two bullets whistled through his coat.

"For God's sake, don't shoot the boy, he is saving the lives of these people." One of the outlaws called for the others to stop shooting. Burton flagged the freight train down only a car's length from the passenger train.

During the excitement, the quick-thinking conductor managed to alert the passengers that robbers were aboard. Everyone reacted with complete calm, according to one eyewitness. The women pulled off their diamonds. One hid her earrings in her stocking, another stuffed her valuables down the front of her dress and covered herself with a shawl. One gentleman hid a gold watch and $100 cash in the water cooler. All were sitting in their seats when Wood, Charlie Ford, and Clarence jumped into the car. Wood carried the grain sack and Charlie followed him, threatening the passengers at gunpoint while they dropped in what possessions they'd been unable to hide. Clarence stood at the door of the car to make certain no one shot the robbers in the back. Among the loot they got was a cake in a basket which Charlie ate as he went through the rest of the cars. He also found a bottle of wine. The man with his money hidden in the water cooler attempted to plead poverty. The robbers naturally did not believe him, cocked a pistol in his face, and he handed over his possessions. Jesse, Dick, and Frank stood guard outside, although Frank climbed into a car near the end of the robbery to see how things were going.

Jesse threatened to shoot the conductor at one point, saying, "This is the revolver that killed Westfall and if you don't look out, you go too." He then stated his name was Jesse James and that he was robbing the Chicago and Alton train because they'd offered reward money for him. Although Jesse gave his name, he was later described as having a dark beard which led some to believe that he was not responsible for the robbery. Evidence would come out later, however, that Jesse apparently dyed his whiskers, which were actually a sandy brown color.

Finally, the gang prepared to leave. Jesse walked up to the brakeman, Burton, and asked if he'd been robbed. Yes, Burton replied, the gang took 50¢, all he had. Jesse handed him $1.50. "This is the principal and interest on your money." Jesse then told the engineer, "Choppy" Foote, that "he was a brave fellow," and handed him two dollars "to drink to the health of Jesse James." The outlaws shook hands with the fireman and even said they'd help remove the rocks from the track, but the engineer hurriedly refused this generous offer. Jesse laughed and the men mounted their horses and rode off.

A witness reported that one of the gang turned and shouted, "This is the last you'll ever see or hear of the James boys!"

Chapter Twenty-Four

Thieves Fall Out

The conviction of Bill Ryan was a shock to Jesse. The days of favorable press coverage and public sympathy for his outlaw deeds were coming to an end. A group of Confederate soldiers even voted to support Crittenden in his fight to bring the outlaws to justice. Detectives had good descriptions to go on now. Everyone knew, for example, that Jesse could be recognized by the missing fingertip on his left hand. The boys decided life would be safer in distant parts, so they split up. Jesse traveled to Kentucky and sent word back to Dick Liddil and Wood Hite to meet him at George Hite's house in Adairville.

Tensions were increasing among the gang. Frank and Jesse separated after the Blue Cut robbery. The brothers probably never saw or even heard from each other again. The exact reasons for the split were never known, but reports indicated that the two got into a bitter fight after the death of Westfall. Frank claimed Jesse had promised him there was to be no killing. It is also likely that Jesse found out about Frank's surrender attempt. This would have been a traitorous act in his eyes. Frank, Charlie Ford, and Clarence Hite started off in the direction of Kentucky, but changed their minds and ended up in Indiana.

Dick Liddil and Wood Hite traveled to Kentucky to meet Jesse, but about a week after their arrival they got into a fight over the division of the loot from the Blue Cut robbery and had "a shooting scrape." Neither one actually hit the other, but

126

Dick left hurriedly. He returned to Missouri, staying with Martha Bolton. Clarence, Charlie Ford, and Frank invited him to travel with them, but he refused.

Clarence and Frank apparently got into some sort of argument, for Clarence broke with the group and headed back to Missouri. He received a letter from Frank in October 1881, saying "I will be at your house on [date]. Respectfully, Joe." In code this meant that the men were to meet at a designated spot in Kentucky, probably the home of Donny Pence. But Clarence wrote back that he'd come down with a sudden illness and wasn't up to traveling. Frank sent back word he was sorry Clarence was sick.

Jesse returned to Kansas City in November, despondent and angry. The gang was now completely broken up. He told his mother that Frank was off south somewhere, and Zerelda immediately jumped to the conclusion that he was dead. Jesse did not bother to correct her. Jesse decided to move his family to Kansas. He contacted Clarence, but his cousin wasn't interested in renewing the friendship. Charlie Ford returned. He now presented himself as Jesse's only friend. Frank had continued on traveling east. Jesse packed up his family once more and they headed out, Charlie Ford driving the wagon while Jesse rode alongside.

They stopped in a small Kansas town (Jesse must have been desperate to consider living in Kansas, home of the old enemy), but Jesse, Jr. remembered that his father didn't like the way the townspeople stared at him. Jesse decided to move to St. Joseph, Missouri. It is highly unlikely that anyone in the little town recognized the outlaw, they were probably just giving him the once over they would any stranger, but this indicates Jesse's growing paranoia. He was becoming more suspicious and distrustful.

After Dick Liddil's return to Missouri, he joined up with Charlie's blond, baby-faced little brother, a kid named Bob Ford. Dick and Bob roamed around the countryside for a few

weeks. They may have pulled a couple of robberies of no particular consequence. They returned to Martha Bolton's, Bob's
sister, late one night in December. But Dick got an unpleasant
surprise when he came down to breakfast. There sat Wood
Hite at the table. Dick, the daring train robber, told Wood "not
to speak to him" because Wood had accused him of being a
thief. Wood denied the charge. The two men grabbed their
guns and headed outside to settle the dispute. (This was the
public version of their quarrel. Most people believed the men
were fighting over the affections of Martha Bolton.) Dick and
Wood faced one another and began blasting away with their
revolvers.

The men were either terrible shots or not very serious about
their argument. According to Dick, both he and Wood fired
four or five times point blank at each other. When the smoke
cleared, Wood had a bullet in his arm and Dick was shot in the
leg. Dick raised his gun to try again. How long the duel might
have lasted is not known. Bob Ford walked out into the yard
and killed Wood with one shot through the head.

The men in the house carried the body upstairs and later
buried it in the woods that night. Dick realized he was in serious trouble. Wood's body was hidden, but quite a few people
living in the Bolton house knew about the murder and were
not known for keeping their mouths shut. If the law didn't find
out, Jesse most certainly would and he would set out to avenge
his cousin's death. Dick believed Jesse suspected him of being
a traitor as well. He was right. Clarence Hite received a letter
from Jesse in December 1881, warning Clarence that Dick was
"in with the detectives."

It is easy to imagine Dick's terror when he heard Jesse's
knock on Martha's door later that month. Charlie Ford was
with him. Jesse smoothly invited Dick to go for a little ride, but
Dick turned down the invitation. "I mistrusted Jesse wanted to
kill me," he said. Dick left Martha Bolton's that night and returned only when he heard Jesse was gone.

Jesse lived in St. Joseph that winter under the name of

Thomas Howard. He was depressed and unhappy, cooped up in the house, rarely daring to ride into town. He wrote Clarence Hite again, telling him he was lonely and asking Clarence to come stay with them for awhile. Clarence refused. Charlie Ford was Jesse's only visitor. Jesse considered him his only friend. The James family lived in a house known as the House on the Hill, because it commanded a full view of the city from all directions—an ideal home for the outlaw. He paid $14 a month rent.

Jesse's son wrote that this time in St. Joseph provided the only clear memories he had of his father. Jesse went around heavily armed at all times, explaining to his little boy that all men wore guns everywhere they went. He kept two horses in the stable, always saddled and ready to ride. In the house was a double-barreled shotgun, a Winchester rifle, a Colt .45 revolver, and a Schofield .45 revolver. If Jesse was going on a trip, he carried both revolvers, the rifle strapped inside an umbrella, and a small valise full of cartridges.

Jesse did not have a job in St. Joseph, but stayed home most of the time, taking occasional trips back to Missouri with Charlie Ford. Ford was introduced as Charlie Johnson, a cousin of the family's. Jesse spent much of his time playing with his children and took his son riding in the country. They rarely went into town, although Jesse, Jr. recalled the day his father decided it would be fun to ride in a big St. Joseph parade, carrying his little son on his horse in front of him. They trotted along directly behind a troop of mounted policemen. But generally they rode in isolated stretches of country. Once Jesse perched his son up on a fence post and demonstrated how he rode in the glorious days when he fought with Bloody Bill. He gripped the reins in his teeth and galloped at full dash toward the excited boy, firing off his pistols in each hand. Jesse also told his son stories of his days with the guerrillas and read, as well as he could, to the child out of Major Edward's book, *Notable Guerrillas.*

But Jesse's home life wasn't always peaceful. Little Jesse remembered a day when the chief of police suddenly appeared outside the House on the Hill with four men. The chief rested his hand on the fence post. Jesse saw the men from the window where he'd been sitting with his son in his lap. He "got up hastily and sat me in a rocking chair, and told me to be very quiet," Jesse, Jr. wrote. His father ran out back to check the horses, then returned, strapped on his revolvers, said something to Zee which the boy could not hear, and then grabbed the rifle out of the closet. Jesse moved near the window and the little boy watched as his father took deadly aim at the police chief. Suddenly the men walked away. Jesse lowered the rifle and nothing more was said. Later they discovered that the police chief was simply showing his friends the view from the House on the Hill. He had no idea who lived there.

While Jesse was having imaginary encounters with law enforcement officers in St. Joseph, Dick Liddil was having problems with real ones. A raid on Martha Bolton's house in January convinced the outlaw that it was only a matter of time before the law got him. He managed to escape out the back door as the officers came in the front, but he later sent his "wife," Mattie Collins, to prosecuting attorney William Wallace to arrange for his surrender. Wallace promised Dick immunity in Jackson County if Liddil turned state's evidence, but nothing further. A woman reported to be Martha Bolton then traveled to Jefferson City to meet with Governor Crittenden. He promised immunity in the state of Missouri for Liddil and others who surrendered. It is likely that Martha Bolton also brought Crittenden word from her brother, Bob. He was interested in collecting $10,000.

Liddil surrendered to authorities on January 24, 1882. Clarence Hite was arrested soon after at his home in Kentucky, just as Jesse had warned. Clarence's arrest made the newspapers, but only a few people knew of Liddil's surrender. It was kept secret. Plans were being made. Clarence immediately confessed and was sentenced to twenty-five years in prison.

The shadows were growing dark around Jesse. He talked of moving once again and even began negotiations with a land agent in Nebraska to buy a farm. But he needed money—and needed it quickly. He and Charlie Ford decided to pull just one more bank job. They had to have three men for the job and Jesse no longer knew anyone he could trust. Charlie had a suggestion—his little brother, Bob Ford.

Chapter Twenty-Five

Jesse's Last Days

Jesse and Charlie rode to the Kansas City area near the end of March. Bob was flattered Jesse thought enough of him to ask him to ride with the gang. He readily agreed to the proposed robbery: a bank at Platte City, Missouri, near St. Joseph. But Bob took Charlie aside and told him he was planning to kill Jesse for the reward money. He told Charlie that Liddil had surrendered and it was being kept secret for fear Jesse would not trust the brothers if the news leaked out. Jesse knew Bob and Dick were friends. Bob told Charlie he had met with detectives and the sheriff's department to arrange the details and that Governor Crittenden had promised them both a full pardon plus the reward money.

Charlie Ford would later claim that he refused to be part of such a dirty scheme, but his brother threatened to kill him along with Jesse if he didn't help. It is more likely that Charlie went along with Bob in hopes of getting his share of the money.

The brothers made their plans. They had to catch Jesse off guard and unarmed if possible. His ability with his revolvers was well known and legend does not exaggerate, according to those who saw him shoot. One story describes Jesse James riding his horse between two trees, firing his revolvers with both hands at a mark in each tree. After he had galloped by at full speed, there was a line of six bullets through the target on one tree and a line of six through the target on the other tree. The

Bob Ford

Ford brothers knew they would never survive a face-to-face shoot-out. They watched for an opportunity, but the former guerrilla had lived with his guns on since he was sixteen. Events of the past few months had made him even more cautious. The Fords waited and watched nervously.

Jesse took the Fords to his mother's home near Kearney to spend the night. But on arrival they discovered that Johnnie Samuels had been shot at a party. He was near death and

Charlie Ford, who committed suicide approximately three years after Jesse's death.

friends were staying with him. The Fords and Jesse hid in the barn until Johnnie's friends left. The twenty-one-year-old man, the same age as Bob Ford, had taken a turn for the better. Jesse moved in, introducing Bob to his mother. Zerelda took an instant dislike to the Ford boy and warned Jesse that he was no good. Jesse just laughed and said, "I'll keep my eye on him."

Jesse visited with his mother that day, sitting on the front porch in the warm spring sunshine. He showed off his shooting ability, knocking a woodpecker out of a tree with one shot. What Bob Ford thought of this exhibition can be imagined. When night came, Jesse and Charlie shared a bed downstairs. Bob Ford slept upstairs in a room that had holes cut out of the wall for rifles to fire through in case the boys ever got in a tight spot. Jesse and the Ford brothers rode off the next day. They stopped at Jesse's half-sister Sallie's home on the way north. She gave him a little dog to take home to Jesse, Jr. Jesse carried the dog in his arms all the way to St. Joseph.

Jesse Woodson James, about 1880.

At Jesse's home the next morning, the two Ford brothers sat down with the family at breakfast. Charlie watched Jesse tease his little son and play with baby Mary. He thought of what they were planning and couldn't eat. Jesse kidded him about his small appetite. The men stayed indoors during the day, since Jesse said it would look suspicious for three men to be seen hanging around the house. The plans for the robbery were made. When Bob Ford complained that he didn't have a reliable gun, Jesse gave him one with pearl handles. He provided Charlie Ford with a new horse. The Fords watched for their chance, but Jesse never took off his guns. He even slept with a revolver under his pillow.

The news of Dick Liddil's surrender broke on March 31, 1882. Jesse had questioned Bob Ford about Dick's whereabouts and Bob claimed he didn't know. According to Bob Ford's account, Jesse picked up the newspaper on the morning of April 3, 1882 and read about Liddil's surrender. He realized Bob had been lying and knew the Fords were there to betray him. He stared at the young man across the breakfast table where Zee was sitting with the children.

"I think Jesse would have killed me, then and there, but he did not want to in front of his family," Bob Ford said.

Jesse smiled at the young man, the warm smile that had made him such a good companion in his youth. But his eyes were the cold blue eyes of the man who gunned down Captain Sheets and murdered the innocent Joseph Heywood.

"Well, Bob, it's all right, anyway," Jesse said, but Ford was not fooled. He knew that the end was near. Jesse moved out of the kitchen into the living room. Bob and Charlie stood watching him. To their amazement, Jesse took off his guns.

"It was the first time in my life I had seen him without that belt on. . . ." Bob Ford said.

Jesse threw his guns carelessly on a cot and turned his back on the Ford brothers. Then he noticed a picture on the wall and muttered something about it needing dusting. He picked

up a feather duster and, keeping his back to the brothers, he
climbed onto a chair and began dusting.

Bob Ford glanced at Charlie and crept out of the kitchen. He
placed himself between Jesse and the guns, drew his revolver—the one Jesse had given him—cocked and aimed it in
one quick motion. Jesse heard the gun cock and turned his
head ever so slightly, but Bob Ford squeezed the trigger. The
bullet struck Jesse in the back of the head, knocking him
forward. His head hit against the wall. He seemed to steady
himself, then swayed and toppled off the chair onto the floor.
The Fords hesitated a moment. Charlie had drawn his gun at
the same time as his brother, but it was obvious another shot
wasn't necessary. Their victim would never rise again.

Zee heard the shot from the kitchen and rushed in to find
her husband near death, blood streaming from his head. Bob
and Charlie were running out the door. She screamed after
them, "Bob, have you done this?"

"I swear to God I didn't," Bob yelled.

"A pistol went off accidentally," Charlie said, then they
leaped over the fence and ran off to dispatch several telegrams.

Zee attempted to wipe the blood from Jesse's face. It was
pouring down too fast. He tried to speak, but collapsed and
died in her arms.

Jesse, Jr. and his little sister, Mary, came in from the kitchen
and saw their father dead on the floor, their mother weeping
over him. Jesse, Jr. later wrote: "Soon after the murder of my
father a great crowd gathered outside the house. My childish
mind imagined that these were responsible for the murder, and
in great anger I lugged from its closet my father's shotgun and
tried to aim it at the people outside, but my mother took it
from me."

One question about Jesse's death remains a mystery. Why
did he take off his guns and turn his back on armed men he
knew were there to betray him? Bob Ford claimed that Jesse
took off his guns to quiet Ford's suspicions and lull him into a
sense of well-being. But this doesn't make sense. Jesse was a

quick-thinking, cold-blooded killer. He knew that Bob Ford was lying in wait for his chance to kill him. Jesse also knew that Bob Ford *had* to kill him—or be killed by him. Maybe there was another reason.

Jesse's life was closing in on him. The gang had broken up. Cole, Bob, and Jim Younger were in prison. John Younger was dead. Bill Ryan was in prison. Clarence Hite was in prison. Dick Liddil had turned traitor. Even his own brother, Frank, had betrayed him. Jesse had no money, a wife and two children to provide for. He discovered that the last two men he trusted were traitors. Had Jesse James reached the conclusion, when he smiled at Bob Ford, that the young man offered him an opportunity to quickly escape from a life that was becoming unbearable?

Chapter Twenty-Six

"I've Got Him, Sure"

Bob Ford sent three telegrams that morning with only one line each, "I've got him, sure." They went to the police chief in Kansas City, Sheriff Timberlake of Clay County, and Governor Crittenden. Back at the house, the coroner had arrived. He questioned Zee. She claimed her name was Mrs. Thomas Howard and her husband had been killed by two men named Johnson. A reporter showed up, trailing after the coroner, to cover what appeared to be a simple murder. He had no idea he would be covering one of the great news stories of the century.

The Ford brothers, their telegrams dispatched, went to the marshal's office to surrender. They were told the marshal and his deputies had gone to the House on the Hill to investigate the report of a shooting. The Fords pushed their way through the crowd outside the house and went inside. The marshal asked them routinely if they could identify the dead man.

"Do you know who that is?" asked Bob Ford, excitedly. "That's Jesse James!"

The marshal was stunned. Zee saw the brothers and began to scream, "Cowards!" at them. The marshal took her into a bedroom and asked her again what her name was. She insisted it was Howard, but finally admitted that the man lying dead on the floor was her husband, Jesse James.

Word flashed through the crowd outside. The reporter latched onto the Ford brothers for an interview. Bob Ford handed the pearl-handled revolvers over to the marshal, saying he shot the famous outlaw and he wanted to surrender. The coroner began to make arrangements for the removal of the body and the inquest. The marshal escorted the Fords to dinner.

When the undertaker arrived and carried the body back to town in a black hearse, crowds followed. Many people were skeptical. A newspaper that very morning had carried a story that Jesse James had been identified robbing a train in Texas. His death had been falsely reported several times already, only to have him turn up alive. But Sheriff Timberlake and other law enforcement officials, who knew Jesse by sight, were already on their way to identify the body.

The undertaker allowed reporters inside to view the body. Scars from two bullet wounds in the chest were discovered, another scar from a bullet was found in the leg. The tip of the middle finger was missing. A photographer was called in. He couldn't take pictures of the body lying flat, so the body was placed on a board and secured with a rope around the legs to keep it from slipping. The photographer got his picture, and many people followed him back to the studio, waiting outside while he developed it so they could get prints. These were sold as fast as he could make them. Reporters wrote that the neatly-groomed man, dressed in a brown cashmere suit, looked more like a doctor or businessman than a desperado.

The inquest was held that afternoon before an audience that was standing-room only. Zee and Bob Ford both identified the body as that of Jesse James. Twenty-four hours later, Zerelda Samuels arrived by train. She was taken to view the body. She stood silently for a moment, then began to wail, "Yes, it is my son. Jesse! Jesse! They have taken you from me. The miserable traitors!" She appeared before the coroner's inquest, reconvened for the purpose. Raising the empty right sleeve, she testified that the body was that of her son. She identified Zee as Jesse's wife and the children as Jesse's children. She was led sobbing out of the courtroom, but the old woman stopped at

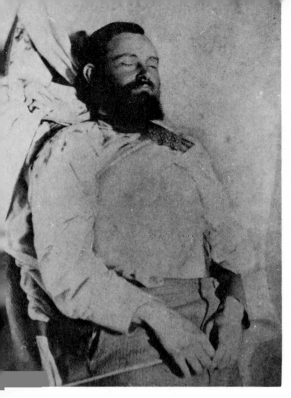

Jesse James on his death bed. Note rope tied around body to keep it in position while photographer took picture. Body had to be propped up because cameras could not take photos from any other angle.

the sight of Dick Liddil, who had been brought up to identify the body. She advanced on him in a fury, screaming, "It would be better if you were in the cooler where my boy is, than here looking at me. . . ." Officers had to restrain her and Dick cowered away, crying, "I did not kill him!"

Zee and her mother-in-law returned to the House on the Hill, which was now being called the Death House. They discovered that souvenir hunters had broken in, stealing guns and jewelry. The two women packed up what few things the James possessed, then moved into the World's Hotel in town to wait until the body was turned over to them for burial. Zee would be forced to auction off nearly all the family's household goods to provide enough money to live on. They kept the feather duster, as well as a cartridge belt that had not been stolen. But they sold almost everything else, including the little dog Jesse brought back for his son.

In Kansas City, "the news of the killing of the famous outlaw created such an excitement on the streets . . . as has not existed since the assassination of President Garfield," commented one newspaper. "Groups gathered on street corners to discuss the matter. . . ." There was widespread disbelief that Jesse was really dead. Crowds gathered at the railroad station to hear the latest news. But testimony followed testimony as Jesse's old friends and enemies all swore to the positive identification of the body. Among them were several old guerrillas, including Harrison Trow and Jim Wilkerson who said, "I ought to know him; I soldiered with him." Dick Liddil remarked, "That's Jess all right. I'd know his hide in a tanyard." Mattie Collins also identified the body along with Zee's uncle and prosecuting attorney William Wallace. People began to believe the notorious outlaw was dead at last.

Crowds lined up and stood for hours outside the undertaker's to view the body. Jesse's face was noted for being strangely calm and tranquil. A bruise above the left eye showed where his head struck the wall. (The bullet did not exit the head and bury itself in the wall, contrary to popular belief. The coroner stated in his report that he removed the bullet, and there is no reason to doubt him. The bullet, in fact, was one of his most treasured possessions from then on and remained in his family for years. The famous bloody mark on the wall, that has been whittled to toothpicks by souvenir hunters, was caused by the force of Jesse's head striking it. The mark has been "authenticated" from time to time with the blood of chickens.)

Mrs. Samuels made arrangements for the funeral, which was to take place at home in Kearney. She bought an expensive casket for $250. According to legend, it was paid for by the police commissioner of Kansas City and Sheriff Timberlake. Soon a hassle started over who had control of the body, the Kansas City police or the St. Joseph police. Finally Governor Crittenden ordered it turned over to the family.

Now that everyone was certain Jesse was dead, questions were being asked about the manner of his death. Piece by piece the story came out. Bob Ford admitted that he had met with Crittenden and police officers in Kansas City and Clay County, offering to "look for" Jesse. These men acknowledged that they knew Ford was with Jesse, but they denied knowledge of the planned assassination. Ford's one-sentence telegram indicates, however, that they were waiting for this news. The role the governor played was particularly criticized, although at first he denied any knowledge of the affair. Later, in his memoirs and in newspaper articles, he boasted of it, referring to the Fords as "my men" and claiming to have accomplished the whole business without costing the taxpayers a cent. Bob Ford was charged and found guilty of murder, but Crittenden immediately pardoned him as arranged. As for the reward money, Crittenden claimed it cost the railroads $20,000 to eliminate Jesse, but Bob Ford certainly did not receive all of it. Charlie later told Mrs. Samuels he only got a "few hundred dollars" himself. Rumor said the money was eventually split between the Fords, Sheriff Timberlake, the Kansas City police chief, the men responsible for catching Ryan and Clarence Hite, and even Governor Crittenden himself.

Governor Thomas Crittenden, 1876. Evidence indicates he ordered the assassination of Jesse James.

The Fords found out that no one loves a traitor, no matter how worthy his cause. Newspapers called for their hanging, there were threats of lynch mobs, and Crittenden was forced to call out the state police to protect them. Newspapers reminded the citizens that a man was considered innocent until proven guilty and added that Jesse had never stood trial for his crimes. They objected to the governor of the state and the police chief taking upon themselves the roles of judge, jury, and executioner. Eastern newspapers commented that this "justice" was typical of the barbaric character of the entire state of Missouri. Members of Missouri's legislature tried to drum up a resolution approving the deed, but it failed to pass. It was appalling to think that a politician had the power to order a man's execution.

Whatever political advantage Crittenden thought he might gain from Jesse's death, he saw dwindle away.

Chapter Twenty-Seven

The Funeral

On April 6, 1882, the body of Jesse James was moved from the undertaker's in St. Joseph to a special train ironically provided by the Hannibal and St. Joseph line. Crowds had waited all night to see the spectacle and trailed after the casket. The family arrived at the depot in a carriage and the crowd had to be restrained from crushing them. While this was occupying the policemen's attention, a man rushed up and tried to whittle pieces off the coffin. The family boarded with members of the police force. The train silently left the station.

The original location of Jesse's grave on the James farm. A recent archaeological excavation discovered the grave was actually dug seven feet deep and also found the original burial casket, a bullet, a tooth, and several small bones.

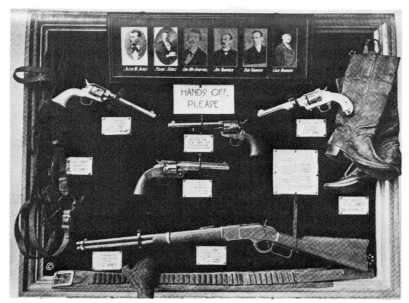

Jesse James' gun collection.

Upon arrival at Kearney, the body was taken to the Kearney House Hotel where it lay in state with the coffin lid open. Hundreds of people traveled to the town from all directions to view the famous outlaw, whose exploits were being flamboyantly retold in all the newspapers. The hotel was only about a block from the depot; all the trains that passed through town stopped long enough for their passengers and crew to get off and view the body.

Later that afternoon, the coffin was carried to the Baptist church where Jesse had been baptized and sung in the choir. The crowds were so large the church was filled and many people stood outside. The minister chose for his text, "Therefore, be ye also ready, for in such an hour as ye think not, the Son of Man cometh." Ironic but appropriate. Zerelda wept and cried out frequently during the service, so the rather trite sermon probably did not attract much attention. It contained no direct

The coffee bean tree in the front yard of the James home in Kearney. The original gravesite of Jesse is marked by an "X." This is also the tree on which Dr. Samuels was allegedly hung.

reference to the outlaw or his family, but exhorted sinners to watch their steps. Afterwards, the minister asked the people not to return to the James' home to view the burial, since Johnnie Samuels was still seriously ill. But another large crowd gathered at the James' farm.

The neighbors dug a grave beneath the coffee bean tree where the Union soldiers had hanged Dr. Samuels eighteen years earlier. Zerelda feared grave robbers or gold-seekers would disturb the grave. Rumors were already spreading that Jesse's gold was being buried with him. Zerelda ordered the men to dig the grave seven feet deep. The casket was lowered into the earth while the widow and mother wept bitterly. Zerelda called upon God for vengeance upon the traitors who murdered her "generous, noble-hearted Jesse." She had the grave covered with rocks taken from a nearby creek bed. (She would later sell these to tourists for 25¢ a pebble, replenishing her stock from the creek.) The crowd drifted away, except for those who stayed behind to comfort the family.

Zee soon returned to St. Joseph and auctioned off what she could. The total sum raised was only $117.65. All sorts of people hounded her, some trying to discover where Jesse had buried his gold, others intent on using her to make their fortunes. She was so desperate for money that she even considered going on the "lecture circuit." But the shy woman couldn't speak in front of an audience, so it was agreed that she would sit on the platform with her children and answer questions following the lecture. This plan fell through and eventually she went to live with relatives in Kansas City.

Bob Ford went on the lecture circuit, after receiving another pardon from Crittenden for the murder of Wood Hite, whose body was discovered after Jesse's death. Ford related to the audience how he killed Jesse James, then he fired off a pistol a few times. But the crowds dwindled. Ford saw to his disappointment that he was seen only as an object of curiosity rather than as a hero. He took a job with P. T. Barnum in a sideshow, but drink and gambling took their toll on the young man. He and Dick Liddil tried running a bar in Las Vegas for a while, but it failed. Dick finally went into racehorse tending and Bob drifted to the mining camps in Creede, Colorado, where he was a success with his barroom tales. On June 8, 1892, Bob got into a fight with a man named Ed Kelly, supposedly a relative of Cole Younger. Kelly shot and killed Ford in a saloon. Bob's brother, Charlie, committed suicide only four years after Jesse's death.

Maybe, after all, Mrs. Samuels' prayers were answered.

Chapter Twenty-Eight

Frank James Comes In

"I am tired of this life of taut nerves, of night-riding and day-riding, of constant listening for footfalls, creaking twigs and rustling leaves and creaking doors; tired of seeing Judas in the face of every friend I know—and God knows I have none to spare. . . ."—Frank James.

The big question during the confusion following Jesse's death was: where was Frank? Rumors put him in St. Joseph gunning for the Fords. Others said he attended the funeral in a disguise and was biding his time to wreak awful vengeance upon his brother's killers. Actually, Frank was living quietly in Lynchburg, Virginia, with Annie and his son, Robert. His wife read the news of Jesse's death in the paper. Frank was shocked and alarmed, according to his statement. He now began negotiations secretly for his own surrender.

No one knows the details. Even Crittenden in his memoirs keeps these terms secret. Frank's old friend, John Edwards, handled the arrangements. Crittenden publicly promised the outlaw a fair trial and protection of his rights in a court of law. Frank agreed to all the terms and returned to Missouri only six months after Jesse's death. Crittenden staged the surrender with the style of a true politician. He was beginning to realize, perhaps, how much Jesse's execution had hurt him politically.

At five o'clock on the afternoon of October 4, 1882, two men went to the governor's office in Jefferson City where Crittenden had assembled a delegation of government officials and reporters, promising them a "Christmas box surprise." He exhibited a letter, purportedly from Frank, which detailed his unhappy life as a hunted criminal. While this was being discussed, Frank and John Edwards walked into the office. It was a dramatic moment and Frank, the lover of Shakespeare, played to an appreciative audience.

Edwards presented the outlaw to the governor, saying, "Governor Crittenden, I want you to meet my friend, Frank James." Frank unbuckled his guns and handed them to the governor stating, "I want to hand over to you that which no living man except myself has been permitted to touch since 1861, and to say that I am your prisoner." The reporters and politicans were thrilled to meet the famous outlaw and gave him a warm welcome. By the time he and Edwards returned to their hotel, hundreds of people had gathered to see him. Governor Crittenden even brought his wife over that evening for a visit.

Arrangements were made to take Frank back to Independence where he would be held on the charge of murdering Detective Whicher. He boarded a train the next day to make the journey, but enthusiastic mobs jammed the railroad stations en

Frank James, around 1890.

The Jackson County Jail

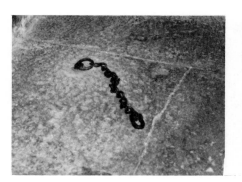

route, forcing the train to stop several times while Frank appeared on the rear platform and waved to the cheering crowd. Another huge crowd saw him in Independence where he met his mother, his wife and child, and the Ralstons. The town's leading citizens even held a reception for Frank where the "wealthiest, most popular and influential men lined up to shake his hand." This included bankers who would have turned dead white at the thought of Frank James stepping into their banks a few days earlier. The governor and his lady attended the gala event and a St. Louis paper bitterly commented that it seemed the state of Missouri had surrendered to Frank James instead of the other way around. Following the reception, Frank was led off to the jail.

Unfortunately, now that the state had Frank, it wasn't sure what to do with him. Prosecuting attorney William Wallace was forced to drop the charge of murdering the detective due to lack of evidence. Finally Daviess County brought charges against Frank for the murder of the stonemason, Frank MacMillan, during the Winston robbery. The charges were made just in time. The governor of Minnesota wanted Frank to fill up a cell next to the Youngers. But Crittenden told him Frank couldn't be delivered to Minnesota until all the Missouri charges were settled. That could take a long time. Frank was now being charged with the murder of Captain Sheets and the robbery at Blue Cut.

While Wallace and the defense gathered their evidence, Frank was being held in the Jackson County jail without bond. Life wasn't too difficult for the outlaw. He was allowed to furnish his cell, complete with a rocking chair. The sheriff regularly took him to the opera or other civic events he thought his prisoner might enjoy. Friends and family visited daily and gifts poured in from all over the United States. Newspapers were filled with editorials either condemning Frank as a coldblooded killer who should be hanged from the nearest tree limb or waving the tattered flag of the Confederacy, calling Frank the man who had never surrendered.

Frank James came to trial in August 1883, in Gallatin, Missouri, for the murder of Fred MacMillan. It would become one of the most famous murder trials in American history.

Chapter Twenty-Nine

Frank James on Trial

The town of Gallatin hadn't seen so many gun-totin' men since the end of the war. Hundreds of people rode in for what was being billed as the most sensational murder trial of the wild west. Half of them supported Frank, the other half wanted to see him swing. Gallatin had never forgotten or forgiven the murder of Captain Sheets. Reporters came from every major newspaper in the United States. Tension was high and nerves taut. Everyone expected trouble; some were hoping for it.

William Wallace knew he was facing the most difficult test in his career, but he had three witnesses he believed would effectively pin the murder of MacMillan on Frank and send him to the gallows. These men were Clarence Hite, Bill Ryan, and Dick Liddil.

Disaster struck on the eve of the trial. Clarence Hite died of tuberculosis and Bill Ryan refused to take the stand. Whether Ryan was threatened or simply decided to remain loyal to his old comrade is not known. All Wallace had now was Liddil and a group of witnesses who could place Frank in the vicinity of the robbery at the time. Wallace knew that Liddil would be immediately challenged by the defense because of his status as a criminal. His testimony might not be allowed. Wallace had other problems, too. Frank's counsel was of the highest caliber. He had eight lawyers, well-known men in Missouri. One would later be in President Woodrow Wilson's cabinet, another would become a federal judge.

Court convened on August 21, but the prosecution announced that it was missing a few witnesses and asked for a continuance until the next day. This was fine with the judge because the old courthouse was packed full of heavily armed men and a muttering crowd waited outside. Judge Goodman announced that for the convenience of those who wanted to attend the famous trial, it would be moved to the Gallatin opera house. Furthermore, the sheriff would hand out tickets to those he decided could enter. All sidearms were to be checked at the door. Anyone caught wearing a gun inside would be dealt with severely. (Wallace ignored this ruling and carried a weapon. He was again receiving threats against his life.) This caused some angry comment, but the judge and the sheriff held firm. There had already been wild rumors of efforts to spring the defendant. Word got out that numerous old feuds, simmering since the bitter days of the war, were going to be settled.

The next day court reconvened in the opera house and the trial began. Judge Goodman sat in a chair on the front of the stage. Behind him sat the ladies of the town and the newspaper reporters. (This arrangement might have been made purposefully to prevent someone from taking a pot shot at His Honor.) The attorneys, the defendant, and the jury were all seated directly in front, facing the stage, in a roped-off area. The jury was made up of relatively young men. Two were ex-Confederate soldiers. The defense was well-pleased with the selection. Wallace reportedly discovered later in the proceedings that the sheriff had selected men for the jury from a list supplied by the defense. This was, of course, denied and nothing could be proven. When Wallace later tried to file for a mistrial, the judge denied his motion before it was even made "to prevent bloodshed."

One hundred and twenty-eight witnesses for both sides were sworn in and Wallace made his opening address to the court. It soon became obvious why he was well-known for his rhetoric:

"There might be some of the jury who admired the exploits of the accused, his chivalric deeds, his expertness, and other characteristics that had made him famous, and such would regard it as a privilege for such a poor and obscure person as MacMillan to be shot down by an individual of such great fame as the accused. . . ."

He recounted the Winston train robbery in graphic detail, gave a brief history of the James gang and a description of how they fled Tennessee following the arrest of Bill Ryan. He called his first witnesses. These were the crew and passengers who were on the train during the Winston holdup. These witnesses established that there had been a robbery and two murders, but none of them could identify the men who fired the shots. Upon cross-examination, one witness said he thought the same man killed MacMillan who killed Westfall (according to both Liddil and Hite, Jesse stated he killed the conductor.)

Sara Hite took the stand. She testified that Frank, Jesse, Wood Hite, and Dick Liddil were all in the Hite home in Kentucky that spring following Ryan's arrest. She described an incident where the boys were being pursued by a posse. They barricaded the house, Dick stood at the front door with a gun, Jesse took aim from a window, and Frank was in the parlor, armed and ready to fire. The posse rode by without incident. Finally, the star witness for the prosecution took the stand—convicted horse thief and confessed train robber, Dick Liddil. The defense immediately objected, claiming Liddil had never been pardoned. Wallace produced what he considered to be pardons. The judge, realizing that the entire case hinged on his decision, adjourned the court to consider the question. In the afternoon, Judge Goodman stated Liddil could testify. He was the opening witness for the second day's hearing.

Wallace's notes reveal that Liddil gave his testimony in an "easy, fluent, matter-of-fact way, and in [a] conversational tone." Dick related how the band reacted to the news of Ryan's arrest, how they met at the Hite home, and how they planned

to return to Missouri with their families. He offered evidence of
this return by stating that Annie James had shipped a sewing
machine to General Jo Shelby with instructions to forward it
to her mother's house. This sewing machine became a crucial
element in Wallace's attempt to prove that Frank moved to
Missouri and not Texas as he would claim. Dick also presented
vivid details of the planning and execution of the Winston
robbery—from Frank's dissatisfaction with the horses stolen to
poor Jesse's toothache. Liddil was weak on only one point. Unfortunately, it was the most important point of the entire case.
Liddil had not seen who shot either MacMillan or Westfall because he had been up front with Clarence holding the engineer
at gunpoint. Liddil stated only that Jesse told him he shot
Westfall and Frank shot MacMillan by accident.

Liddil's cross-examination continued into the third day. He
was calm and unshaken in the presence of the defense lawyers
who continually tried to trap him into making a mistake. He
added detail after detail to his previous testimony, describing
places the gang stopped for meals or had horses shod. He ob-
viously impressed the court with his coolness.

Wallace called more witnesses to the stand after Liddil, who
identified Frank as being in their homes or places of business
before or after the Winston robbery. These included the Bolton
family who went into great detail over the murder of Wood
Hite (all of which the defense brought out to discredit Liddil).
But the most damaging testimony came from the Reverend
Benjamin Matchett. Reverend Matchett lived three miles from
Winston and positively identified Frank as the man who
stopped by his house with another man on July 14, 1881. (The
robbery occurred on July 15.) Frank, who had called himself
"Willard," impressed the minister by his discussions of well-
known contemporary authors like Robert Ingersoll. Reverend
Matchett even loaned "Willard" a book of Ingersoll's lec-
tures to read before bed. The next day, "Willard" quoted
Shakespeare at length for the admiring minister. There were

probably few men in Missouri at the time who could quote Shakespeare from horseback.

Other witnesses remembered Jesse and his toothache, including the man who drove him to town to put him on the train. They all positively identified Frank as being with the gang. The defense could shake none of them on this important point, although Frank had been wearing "burnside" whiskers at the time.

"Is not the truth, the truth?" to quote Falstaff.

Chapter Thirty

General Jo Shelby

The state rested its case on the fifth day of the trial. Although they had presented an overwhelming amount of evidence proving Frank James was in the vicinity of the robbery and that he had been riding with Jesse James and the gang, Wallace did not have one person, other than Dick, who could swear that Frank had actually been on the train. No one had seen him fire the gun that killed MacMillan.

The defense followed the classic line that had been appearing in the newspapers—Frank was considered an outlaw simply because he fought on the losing side of the Civil War. Defense attorney Philips condemned Dick Liddil as a coward and a murderer who would say anything to save his own craven hide. He insisted that the witnesses who said they saw Frank around Winston actually saw a man who greatly resembled Frank—Wood Hite. They would prove Frank was in Texas at the time of the robbery.

The highlight of the sixth day's session was the appearance of General Jo Shelby. There was no other man more admired by Missouri rebels and the crowds were eagerly awaiting his statement. Newsmen had interviewed him and run the story of Frank saving his life and Jesse saving the hired man.

The day he was due to testify, Shelby had lunch with his old friend Major Edwards. Both men decided to have a little bourbon with their lunch; they finished lunch and continued drinking bourbon. The General drank himself into a rage at the thought of his old friend standing trial for murder and entered the opera house "with the stride of a dragoon, and with a savage glare in his eyes which promised trouble."

He sat down in the witness chair and the defense attorney asked him to state his name for the record. Shelby ignored him. The general glanced around the courtroom and finally asked where the judge was. He was told to look on the stage. Shelby located His Honor and wanted to shake hands with him. The audience snickered. Judge Goodman shifted uncomfortably in his chair and ordered the witness to dispense with formalities and answer the question. But now Shelby couldn't find the jury and insisted on knowing where they were. The attorney pointed them out. The general stood and gave them a courtly bow which delighted the audience.

Finally Shelby settled down and gave his place of residence. But everyone in the courtroom knew by now that he was drunk and in a rare mood. William Wallace came forward to cross-examine the witness and Shelby's eyes glittered with hatred. Wallace had been a Confederate soldier and Shelby considered the man a traitor to his beloved cause for prosecuting an ex-Confederate. Shelby answered Wallace's questions sullenly. He had seen Jesse and Dick Liddil in 1881, but Frank was not with them. Jesse said Frank was in poor health and had gone south. At this point the general suddenly recognized Frank James sitting in the defendant's chair. He stood up and called out, "Where is my old friend and comrade in arms? Ah, there I see him! Allow me, I wish to shake hands with my fellow soldier. . . ." The appalled judge banged for order in the courtroom, shouting out, "No, sir, not now."

Wallace continued his questioning. Shelby remembered seeing Frank's wife, but wasn't sure when. He knew nothing about the sewing machine. When Wallace pointed out that Shelby's initials were on the shipping bill, Shelby angrily asked Wallace if he was accusing him of lying and wanted to know if he cared "to make a personal matter of it," in other words, challenging him to a duel. The judge ordered him to calm down, but Shelby continued to refuse to respond to Wallace's questions. The attorney for the defense finally suggested that the general's testimony "be deferred," but Shelby insisted that he be allowed to continue.

Judge Goodman warned Shelby that his "demeanor would not be tolerated" and he promised to behave. But Wallace's next question about Liddil set him off again. "I saw him like a viper, curled up in a rocking chair," sneered the general. When asked if he hadn't tried to kill Liddil in town, Shelby accused the town marshal of lying about him and worked himself into such a state that the judge threatened to fine him $50. The general's testimony ended with a description of treating Frank in his home when he was sick in 1872. The general was allowed to step down to the great relief of the judge and attorneys.

But Shelby wasn't finished yet. He again asked permission to shake hands with Frank. When the judge refused, Shelby called out loudly, "God bless you, old fellow," as he left the courtroom. When court reconvened the next day, the attorney for the defense stated that Shelby had a few words to say to the court. Judge Goodman allowed him to come forward, no doubt vastly relieved to see the General was sober. Shelby apologized for his behavior to the court, but refused to apologize for anything he said "to others," meaning Wallace.

Judge Goodman reprimanded him, stating that a man of Shelby's reputation must have known that "to enter a court of justice in such a condition . . . was not only an insult to the court, but was an act of the greatest injustice toward the man who was on trial for his life. . . ." The judge fined Shelby $10 and warned him not to threaten Attorney Wallace further. Shelby paid the fine, but ignored the warning.

Someone handed Wallace a note that afternoon. It said Shelby had vowed to kill him on sight as soon as he left the courtroom. Wallace had been receiving threats almost daily, but this was different. Shelby was a man of his word and his violent temper was legendary. Wallace left the opera house that afternoon with his arms full of law books to prepare himself for the next day's session. The dirt streets were muddy, for it had rained that day. A plank lay across the street, which was otherwise impassable. Wallace set his foot on the plank and started across. He saw someone else crossing from the other side. That person was General Shelby. The attorney did not flinch or step aside, for he had been a soldier too. But there is no doubt William Wallace expected to die that day on the streets of Gallatin.

Shelby, however, simply lifted his hat, bowed, and said, "You pass first, Mr. Wallace."

The trial continued.

Chapter Thirty-One

Frank Takes the Stand

Shelby's act was a hard one to follow, but the defense had a few more interesting witnesses waiting in the wings of the opera house. One testified that Martha Bolton said Frank was trying to lead an honest life. He was a different man from Jesse; Frank would go away and settle down but when Jesse'd turn up, he'd find himself surrounded by detectives and have to flee. Johnnie Samuels was called to the stand and swore that Frank had not been home during the Winston robbery. Jesse had told the family that Frank was in the south for his health. Johnnie further stated that Wood Hite and Frank bore a striking resemblance to each other, but, on cross-examination, Johnnie could not recall that he had ever heard Wood Hite quote Shakespeare.

Zerelda, who had become almost as notorious as her boys, took the stand. Once again she raised the empty sleeve to swear the oath. She claimed she had not seen Frank for seven years and believed he was dead. She insisted that Jim Cummins was the "other man" in the gang.

The defense next called the Parmers to the stand. Alan Parmer, Frank's brother-in-law, ex-guerrilla fighter, and former gang member, testified that he was working away from home in the summer of 1881, but on returning for a visit in August he found Frank staying there. (The Parmers lived in Texas.) Parmer stayed home only a few days, then left again to continue working on the railroad around Fort Worth. Frank was gone when he came back in September. He could not remember what Frank was wearing at the time, but described his horse. His wife, Frank's sister Susie, took the stand. She testified that Frank arrived in Wichita Falls in June 1881. He told her he and Jesse had been afraid to stay in Tennessee after Ryan's arrest. He spoke of trying to arrange surrender terms with the governor of Missouri. Frank stayed until the first of July, then left, and returned in August. (The robbery was July 15.)

None of the neighbors knew Frank was staying with the Parmers, Susie told the court, because her brother would hide either upstairs or in the cellar if anyone appeared. Susie said Frank left her house in September and she had not seen him since. Neither she nor her husband knew Clarence or Wood Hite or Dick Liddil. Apparently the defense called the Parmers to refute claims that Frank was in Missouri months before the robbery, although it is interesting to note the fact that he could have been at his sister's, ridden north, committed the Winston robbery, and ridden back to Texas in the time allowed by her testimony. He also left Texas in time to commit the Blue Cut holdup that fall.

Two other witnesses followed the Parmers, but they did not reveal anything significant. Then the moment came that everyone had been waiting for—Frank James was called to testify in his own defense.

Frank gave a brief history of his life in Tennessee. He stated that he met Ryan in Jesse's company and only met Jesse by accident in a grain store in the spring of 1878. Throughout his testimony, Frank implied that he had little to do with Jesse or his friends; that he did not approve of them; and that he left Nashville to escape their company. He said he feared Ryan's arrest because he knew the outlaw would tell lies about him, endangering his life by making him a wanted man.

Frank admitted he traveled to the Hites' with Jesse, Dick, and Wood. He remembered the incident with the detectives, only in his version he pleaded with Dick and Jesse not to kill anyone and watched from the parlor out of curiosity. He denied entering into a conspiracy with Dick and Jesse to return to Missouri for the purpose of robbery. He even tried to prevent Jesse from coming back, saying, "You know there is no protection for my mother and family in the state of Missouri, let alone for you, and I would never go there." Frank even gave some fatherly advice to young Dick, telling him to get a steady job and he'd "have much more money at the end of the year than if he put in his time galloping around the country."

The boys did not take Frank's advice, however, and left for Missouri. Frank claimed he went to Texas to stay with his sister. His health was poor, the hard work he'd done over the past few years (ten hours a day) had injured his lungs. He admitted leaving his sister's in July, but said he only spent a few days in the Indian territory, Oklahoma. He read about the Winston robbery in the newspaper.

He told about sending Annie to General Shelby in the spring to arrange for his surrender and that he instructed her to go on to California if Shelby was not encouraging. He then met her when she returned in the fall and they traveled along the James River, stopping at various towns looking for work. He read about the Blue Cut robbery in the paper. He was in Lynchburg when he heard of Jesse's death from Annie. His response was, "My god, where and how and who killed him?" He began negotiating his own surrender shortly afterwards.

Mr. Wallace rose for cross-examination and asked the obvious: if Frank wanted to part company with Jesse and Ryan, why did he return to Kentucky with them. Frank replied, "I went because I wanted to go there to see friends and to help in getting rid of these people [Jesse and Dick]." Mr. Wallace took Frank back every step of the way through Kentucky, Tennessee, Texas, and on east. Frank gave as good as he got, coming up with details about where he stayed, who he was with, etc. The only place he faltered was on the Texas visit, particularly during the time he was gone from his sister's house. He said he was staying with a friend in the Indian territory, but refused to give out the friend's name or location because it might incriminate him. When asked why he could remember names, dates, and places while traveling through Virginia, but not Texas, Frank replied that he was "alone and anxious" in Texas.

The defense rested its case following Frank's testimony, and Wallace recalled several witnesses in rebuttal. First called were several friends of the man who claimed Frank James was not aboard the train. These men all swore that this gentleman told them the robbers were fifteen feet tall and carried revolvers four feet long. The next witness recalled was Sara Hite. She said Frank and Wood did not resemble each other in the slightest and that Wood probably never read a book in his life, much less Shakespeare. She also testified that Jesse had arrived at their house in the spring of 1881 seeking Jim Cummins with the intention of killing him. This made it unlikely that Jim would have been part of the gang that robbed the Winston train. Other men were called to refute testimony that Frank resembed Wood Hite. Then it was time for the judge's instructions to the jury.

Although the defense did not like the judge's instructions, they read very fairly to the defendant. The judge reminded the jury that they had to believe beyond a reasonable doubt that Frank had been on the train, that he had committed a robbery, and that during the commission of the robbery, he killed Mac-Millan, willfully, deliberately, premeditatedly, or with malice aforethought. The jury was told to give Liddil's testimony the credit they felt it deserved, remembering that he was an accomplice in the crime. The attorneys for the defense asked to read their own set of instructions in which they emphasized that the state had not been able to prove positively that Frank was on the train.

Then it was time for the lawyers' summations to the jury. This proceeding took three days. All the speeches (every lawyer on the case gave a speech) were filled with the vivid rhetoric so popular with orators and writers of the time. Only two speeches were recorded in Wallace's notes, his own and that of Judge Philips, counsel for the defense. Both are classic examples of overblown rhetoric and also reveal the divergent opinions of the public in regard to the James boys.

Philips spoke ahead of Mr. Wallace, who was the final speaker. He began by hailing Frank as a soldier fighting for the lost cause. He referred to the James gang as "the last remnant in the state of unreconciled and unaccepted parties to the local predatory struggle. . . ." He graphically described the flight from Missouri to Tennessee because, "the ghosts of war hung around his footsteps in Missouri." He dwelt on the blissful domestic life of Frank and Annie and how Frank worked to earn an honest living. Then arrived "the slimy serpent of evil"— Dick Liddil—who began to rob and pillage with Jesse, Bill Ryan, and Jim Cummins. He reminded the jury how Frank had tried to break with the gang and emphasized how no one could positively identify him at the scene of the crime. The defense spent a great deal of time running down Dick Liddil's character, insisting that such a man could not be believed. Philips finally ended a speech that ran forty-two printed pages and lasted four hours by calling upon the jury to "let your verdict be a loyal response to the evidence and the spirit of the law; and as true manhood ever wins tribute, when the passion of the day is past, and reason has asserted her dominion, you will be honored and crowned."

Wallace began by bringing in the widows of Fred MacMillan and the conductor Westfall. The women, dressed in black with their little children clinging to their skirts, sat in the courtroom while Wallace made his final speech. It was a pathetic scene, the women and children sobbed as they listened to the lawyer's impassioned plea to convict the murderer. He denounced the "lost cause" business, stating that the ghosts of Confederate soldiers were rising from their graves at this sacrilege. He dwelt at great length upon the terms willfully, pre-meditatedly, etc. for the jury and then when on to describe the robbery in bloody detail. He told that Westfall made "some motion thus . . . to defend himself . . ." and "Jesse James—quick as a tiger for his victim—pulls the cruel trigger, and Westfall goes reeling down the aisle to the rear end of the car; as he goes the firing at him is continued. He opens the door, struggles out, and falls dead from the train . . . dead on duty!" Then he described MacMillan's death, his widow crying in the background, "the whizzing ball of the idle, roving assassin meets the sweated brow of hard-working Frank MacMillan. . . ."

So impassioned was Mr. Wallace and so pitiful was the sight of the women that applause resounded through the opera house, and the judge furiously ordered the spectators to re-member where they were. Wallace concluded by calling for "the God of the widow and the fatherless—of MacMillan's wife and child—[to] come into your hearts, and guide you to a righteous verdict in this case." Wallace's entire speech ran eighty-nine printed pages. It ended at 12:30 P.M., probably be-ginning when court convened that morning. Applause marked the close of his speech and the jury retired. They came back at 4:00 P.M. and the foreman read the verdict.

"State of Missouri v. Frank James—murder: We, the jury in the above entitled cause, find the defendant not guilty as charged in the indictment. [Signed] Wm. T. Richardson, Fore-man."

Frank embraced Annie while the audience applauded. He was a free man—but not for long.

Chapter Thirty-Two

An Old Man
on a Train

Frank faced other charges in Missouri, and Minnesota was still waiting for him eagerly. Alabama wanted him too, for the Muscle Shoals robbery. But politics entered the picture again, and such complicated political and legal maneuverings went on for four years that it would be difficult to trace them here. Frank was turned over to Jackson County for the Blue Cut robbery, but Wallace was forced to drop the case when a supreme court ruling made Liddil's testimony inadmissible without a full pardon from the governor, which Crittenden refused to issue. Frank was sent to Alabama where he faced federal charges for the robbery of the paymaster, but once again, no witness could positively identify Frank as being with the gang. Dick Liddil testified during that trial, but he turned nasty under cross-examination without the brilliant Wallace to keep him under control. The Southern jury found it easy to dismiss his testimony from their minds and Frank was acquitted. A sheriff arrested him again right in the courtroom and Frank was returned to Missouri on charges of robbing the Otterville train. Rumor said that the Minnesota law officers had been going to arrest Frank, so Missouri beat them to it.

Frank was released on bond, since the charge did not involve murder, and he traveled around the state, acting as a starter for local horse races. He drew large, admiring crowds.

171

During this time, Crittenden came up for reelection as Missouri's governor and lost. Despite reports that this was due to his foul treatment of Jesse, it was more likely that the man lost simply because his own party disliked him and he had failed to bring Missouri into more progressive times.

The new governor was John Marmaduke, who had been a general in the Confederate army and fought with Shelby and Price. There was now no doubt in anyone's mind that Minnesota would never see Frank James standing in their dock. On February 22, 1885, the charges at Otterville were dropped two days before the trial was scheduled to begin. The reason given was the death of the major witness. Frank James was free at last.

No doubt many of the readers of dime novels who had been entertained by wild stories of the James brothers hoped Frank would once again hit the outlaw trail. But the forty-two-year-old man returned to the peaceful life he had once known in

Teddy Roosevelt on the Paseo, Kansas City, Missouri. The date is uncertain. Frank James was an admirer of Roosevelt. Legend has it that because of this admiration, he was not allowed to attend the Quantrill guerrilla reunions after the turn of the century.

Quantrill reunion, around 1900. Note the Quantrill portrait in the foreground. Frank James is thought to be the fourth from the right, back row.

Tennessee and never deviated from it. He had promised Major Edwards that he would not take to the lecture circuit, although he was flooded with requests and assured that he could make his fortune several times over. He enjoyed starting horse races for county and state fairs, and this is the only time he ever fired his gun. He lived in various places in Missouri and Texas, holding down regular jobs and maintaining his lifestyle in modest settings. He was a shoe salesman, worked in a dress factory, was a horse tender, and a door keeper in a vaudeville theater.

Frank avoided reporters and generally refused interviews, although he gave one that is now famous to a St. Louis reporter named O'Neill following his surrender. He never discussed his relations with Jesse or his life as an outlaw. He did, however, like to talk about his days with the guerrillas and Quantrill, claiming that the guerrillas were totally justified in all the actions they took and never doubting that his captain had been a great man. Frank attended the Quantrill reunions, which started in 1889, and were held in the Independence area afterwards. These featured a portrait of their old commander and as

Bob James, son of
Frank James.

many of the veterans and their families attended as possible. They made up a roll of the men who fought with him and recalled the old days with affection. Many were now professionals, doctors, lawyers, and one was even a lieutenant-governor of a Southern state.

Major John Edwards died in 1889 of complications resulting from alcoholism, which had plagued him all his life. He was still dedicated to the lost cause; one of his last acts was to draw up a petition for the release of the Younger brothers. Various other powerful figures in Missouri were also working for their release from the Minnesota penitentiary. Cole Younger had become a model prisoner, very religious, and impressed touring visitors with his story of how he went from sinner to saint. Minnesota eventually decided to release the boys, but Bob Younger died of tuberculosis in 1889. Cole and Jim were freed in 1901, but they had no legal rights and could not leave the state. Jim committed suicide in 1902, despondent because he was not allowed to marry the girl he loved. The wound he suffered in the Northfield robbery had caused him to lose most of his jaw. He had been living on nothing but liquids for years. Following Jim's death, Cole was given a full pardon and he returned to Missouri.

He immediately went on the lecture circuit. His talk was titled "Crime Does Not Pay," varied with "What Life Has

Taught Me." He gave one of these speeches at a Quantrill reunion where it was well received. It was inevitable that he and Frank join up again. In 1903 they started a wild west show, but it was not a tremendous success. Cole, by the terms of his pardon, was not permitted to participate in the show, but he sat in the audience and visited with the crowd. Frank rode in the stagecoach that was robbed in the finale. Ironically, the biggest problem the two notorious outlaws faced was petty thieves who hung around the shows and bilked the "suckers" out of their money. Frank was even jumped by a couple of thugs, but he called out to Cole that "they'd take care of them like they did in the old days," and the men left hurriedly. Frank was finally forced to write local authorities, begging for better police protection.

He eventually gave up the road life and returned to farming, living off and on at the old James' farm. He gave tours of the place for 25¢ to 50¢. His mother continued to live on the farm with Dr. Samuels, who was now a semi-invalid. In 1902 she made the decision to have Jesse reburied in the family cemetery, no longer fearing grave robbers would steal his body. One Sunday, Jesse, Jr., now twenty-seven years old, brought a coffin and two men who were professional grave-openers. They

Frank James and hound dog in buggy, around 1914, just before Frank's death.

began to dig up the grave in the yard. A large crowd gathered. Several men had come forward, claiming to be the real Jesse James, all declaring that the shooting in St. Joseph had been a hoax. The family had even been to court to counter their claims. Reporters were on the scene. Everyone wondered whether or not a body would really be found in the coffin. If so, whose body was it?

Seven feet down they came to the casket. When they lifted it out, the bottom gave way and a skull tumbled out to the pleasurable horror of the crowd. The grave digger handed it to young Jesse. There was the bullet hole in the back of the head and young Jesse identified the skull as that of his father from several gold teeth which he remembered. They arranged the body in a new casket. A nickel plate on top read simply "Jesse James." Several old Quantrill veterans accompanied the casket to its new location at the Mt. Olivet Cemetery in Kearney. Frank James removed his hat and put his arm around his mother as the casket was lowered into the ground. There was no ceremony and no one spoke.

Newspapers carried the story that the body had been identified as that of Jesse James, but even as late as the 1950s, men still came forward, claiming to be the famous outlaw. One man even claimed to be the real Frank James while the real Frank

Jesse's grave in Kearney, Missouri.

James home in Kearney, 1980. Restoration is underway.

was still living. There can be no doubt that Jesse was actually killed in 1882. A conspiracy to stage his murder, then keep his true identity secret to escape the law, would have been far too complex to carry out and would have involved too many people lying about the identification of the body, including Jesse's enemies as well as his friends.

Zerelda continued to live on the old farm. Her husband, Dr. Samuels, died in a state hospital in 1908. The rope burns could still be seen on his neck. Sometimes Frank and Annie lived with her, but in 1911 they moved for a short time to a farm in Oklahoma. Zerelda died on a train trip to visit them in 1911. She was eighty-seven years old. She was buried next to Jesse, as she had requested. Dr. Samuels and her little son, Archie, are buried next to her.

Jesse's wife and children lived in Kansas City, receiving aid from relatives and friends, among them Thomas Crittenden, son of the governor. Jesse, Jr. managed to get himself involved in a train robbery in 1898, creating quite a sensation in Kansas City. He was acquitted in a jury trial and there is little doubt that he was framed. Following this, young Jesse became a lawyer, practicing in Kansas City. He moved to California, however, to finally escape the complications of living in Missouri—the son of Jesse James.

The kitchen area in the James home following restoration in 1980.

Frank returned to the James' farm with Annie. His son Robert was living quietly in St. Louis. Frank continued to attend the Quantrill reunions, although he nearly got into a fight during one when he expressed admiration for Teddy Roosevelt, the Republican candidate for president. If Frank had said he admired Abraham Lincoln, his old companions could not have been more shocked. A friend told Teddy when the president

Mrs. Frank James (Annie Ralston), around 1927. The photograph was taken at 11004 East 20th Street, Independence, Missouri (the Abston home).

The grave of Frank and
Annie, Independence,
Missouri.

visited St. Louis that the notorious outlaw was a fan. Teddy
was reportedly charmed and even considered inviting Frank to
lunch at the White House. This never came about, however.

On February 18, 1915, Frank James died quietly in the old
home that held so many memories. He was seventy-two years
old. His wife, Annie, was at his side. Fearing that his body
would be exhumed, like Jesse's, he left instructions to be cre-
mated. When Annie died in 1944, after a life of seclusion on
the old farm, she and Frank were buried together in her family's plot in Independence, Missouri. The graves are located in
a small area under the shadow of a tree in Hill Park, shut off
from the world by a stone wall. The grave marker reads simply, "Alexander F. James."

Cole Younger died one year later, in 1916. With him died

The grave of Jesse and
Zee in Kearney, Mis-
souri.

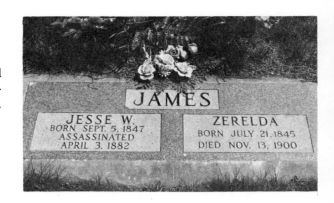

the last of the wild west outlaws, although Butch Cassidy and the Sundance Kid were still supposedly roaming South America. (Butch was born in 1866, the year the James gang robbed the Liberty bank.) The days of the cowboy, the lawman, and the outlaw were passing into romantic glory.

These men and women had held their own destiny in their hands. They'd been responsible to no man, to no law. Most died violently like Jesse—the Dalton brothers shot down in Coffeyville, Belle Starr ambushed on a lonely road, the Clantons killed at the O.K. corral, Billy the Kid shot to death by a friend.

One day in the 1900s, the train was passing through Glendale. It was very quiet in the passenger car when the silence was broken by an old man's voice. "Sure hope we're not robbed," he chuckled with a gleam in his eye.

The conductor shook his head admiringly.

"That's Frank James," he commented to a passenger in a low voice.

Chapter Thirty-Three

Jesse and the Widow

The most famous legend about Jesse James is quite possibly a true one. It has all of Jesse's style and nothing exists to refute it. It is a perfect example of how Missourians viewed their folk hero and is therefore highly suitable for ending the account of his life.

Frank, Jesse, and the Younger boys were riding through Missouri one beautiful summer's day, looking for a place to stop for lunch. They came upon an isolated farmhouse and stopped. Tying their horses outside, they knocked on the door and asked the young woman who answered it if she could fix lunch for them. She said yes and invited them inside. The men sat in the living room, which was very plainly furnished, to wait for their meal.

Jesse noticed that the young woman was crying, however, while she cooked. He saw that her small children were unusually quiet and did not run around and play like other children, but sat huddled in a corner. Finally he could stand the woman's weeping no longer and asked her what the matter was.

She was a widow, she replied. Her husband had died in the war. Now her farm, which was all she had left, was being foreclosed by a heartless old skinflint who had long had his eye on her land. She had no place to go and no money. She and her children were being turned out into the wilderness.

The men were all touched by her story and ate the simple meal in silence, after murmuring what words of consolation they could come up with. But Jesse ate thoughtfully and finally asked how much money it would take to pay off the mortgage.

"Eight hundred dollars," she sobbed.

"When is he coming?" asked the outlaw.

"This afternoon," replied the widow.

Jesse continued to eat in silence.

When the meal ended, Jesse stood up and announced that he was going to loan the woman the money. She stared at him in amazement, then burst into tears again and said she could never repay him. He told her not to mind that and muttered something about getting his money back when he passed this way again.

"But there's one thing you must do," he warned the woman. "You must get this man to sign a receipt." He asked Frank to draw one up for her. Then he gave the woman the money and the men prepared to ride off. "Don't tell him anyone has been here," the men added.

"By the way," Jesse asked. "What will this man be driving?"

"A carriage with one horse," the woman answered, puzzled.

"And what road will he take back to town?" Frank put in.

She told them. The brothers rode away with the grateful woman's blessing.

The old skinflint showed up, eager to get the pretty little house and the valuable farmland. He was furious when the widow handed him the money, but there was nothing he could do. He signed her receipt in bitter anger and drove away, the eight hundred dollars in his pocketbook.

Suddenly five armed men blocked his path.

"Hand over your money and your valuables," said one of the outlaws.

The skinflint pulled out the pocketbook and handed it over in terror.

The bandits grabbed it and rode off. One stopped, turned around, and lifted his hat.

"My name's Jesse James!" he called out, waving his hat with a flourish.

Then he dashed off into the brush.

In Loving Remembrance of My Beloved Son,
JESSE W. JAMES.
Died April 3, 1882
Aged 34 Years, 6 Months, 28 Days.
Murdered by a Traitor and a Coward Whose
Name is Not Worthy to Appear Here.

Framed inscription that hangs on a wall in the James' home in
Kearney, Missouri.

Bibliography

Brownlee, Richard S. *Gray Ghosts of the Confederacy: Guerrilla Warfare in the West, 1861–1865,* Baton Rouge, LA: Louisiana State University Press, 1958.

Burch, John P., *Charles W. Quantrell* (sic). *A True History of His Guerrilla Warfare on the Missouri and Kansas Border During the Civil War of 1861 to 1865* as told by Captain Harrison Trow. Vega, Texas: J. P. Burch, 1923.

Castel, Albert. *General Sterling Price and the Civil War in the West.* Baton Rouge, LA: Louisiana State University Press, 1968.

Connelley, William Elsey. *Quantrill and the Border Wars.* New York: Pageant Book Company, 1956.

Croy, Homer. *Jesse James Was My Neighbor.* New York: Duell, Sloan and Pearce, 1949.

Hale, Donald R. *They Called Him Bloody Bill: The Life of William Anderson, Missouri Guerrilla.* Clinton, Missouri: Donald Hale, 1975.

Hale, Donald R. *We Rode With Quantrill: Quantrill and the Guerrilla War as told by the Men and Women Who Were With Him with A True Sketch of Quantrill's Life.* Clinton, Missouri: Donald Hale, 1975.

James, Jesse, Jr. *Jesse James, My Father: The First and Only True Story of His Adventures Ever Written.* New York: Frederick Fell, Inc., 1957 (originally published in 1899).

McCorkle, John. *Three Years With Quantrill: A True Story.* New York: Buffalo-Head Press, 1966.

O'Flaherty, Daniel. *General Jo Shelby, Undefeated Rebel.* Chapel Hill, NC: The University of North Carolina Press, 1954.

Settle, William A., Jr. *Jesse James Was His Name,* Lincoln, Nebraska: University of Nebraska Press, 1977 (originally published 1966).

The Trial of Frank James for Murder with Confessions of Dick Liddil and Clarence Hite and History of the "James Gang." Foreword by James D. Horan. New York: Jingle Bob/Crown Publishers, Inc., 1977 (originally published in 1898).

Wybrow, R. J. "Jesse's Juveniles," The English Westerner's *Brand Book.* Vol. 12, No. 1, October 1969, London.

Wybrow, R. J. "When Lightning First Struck," The English Westerner's *Brand Book.* Vol. 13, No. 3, April, 1971, London.

INDEX

About the Authors

Margaret Edith (Weis) Baldwin was born in 1948 in Independence, Missouri. She graduated from the University of Missouri, Columbia, with a dual degree in Creative Writing and History. Ms. Baldwin works for Herald Publishing House as director of the trade division, Independence Press, and is advertising director. She has worked for Herald House for ten years. The author is married to Robert Baldwin, State Trooper with the Missouri State Highway Patrol and has two children, David and Elizabeth, and three cats. She is currently a founding member of the Friends of the James Farm in Kearney and on the Board of Directors of that association. She also belongs to the Great Alkali Plainsmen, a scion society of the Baker Street Irregulars, located in Kansas City, Missouri. The group is dedicated to studying the works of Sherlock Holmes and Dr. Watson.

William Patrick O'Brien was born in 1950 in Independence, Missouri. He was graduated from Central Missouri State University, Warrensburg, Missouri with a degree in History and English Literature. His graduate work was completed at the University of Missouri/Kansas City in 1979, at which time he was awarded a Master of Arts degree in American History and Archival Science. He was admitted to Phi Alpha Theta, Pi Phi Chapter, Kansas City, Missouri, a history honors fraternity, in 1978. Mr. O'Brien is presently employed as Historic Preservation Officer for the City of Independence, Missouri, where he has worked for the past four and one half years. In addition to his work for the City of Independence, Mr. O'Brien also has amateur interest in the piano and is especially interested in ragtime and early jazz.